Regina Caeli

The Blessed Mother's Miraculous Signs in Naju, Korea

Mary's Touch By Mail

In conformity with the decrees by Pope Urbanus VIII, the Publisher recognizes and accepts that the final authority regarding the revelations in Naju, Korea, rests with the Holy See of Rome, to whose judgment we willingly submit.

The decree of the Congregation for Propagation of the Faith A.A.S. 58, 1186 (approved by Pope Paul VI on October 14, 1966) states that the Imprimatur is no longer required on publications that deal with new revelations, apparitions, prophecies or miracles, provided that they contain nothing contrary to faith and morals.

Published by:

Mary's Touch By Mail
P.O. Box 1668
Gresham, OR 97030 U.S.A.

Spiritual Director: Rev. Robert J. Billett, C.M.F.

Cover photo: Fr. Raymond Spies holds the Eucharist that miraculously descended to the Chapel in Naju on August 27, 1997, before the Blessed Mother's statue.

Contents

Appendix

Dedication

We dedicate this book to St. Andrew Kim (1821-1846),
the first Korean priest, and all other Catholic martyrs in Korea.

Foreword

About ten years ago, in August 1991, I was in Lourdes, France, with my eleven year-old son on our first pilgrimage ever to a Catholic shrine in Europe. We were filled with joy to be there where our beloved Heavenly Mother actually and personally visited Bernadette in 1858 and gave extremely important messages to the whole human race through her. We were also deeply impressed by the beauty and enormous scale of the shrine. One of the souvenirs we bought in Lourdes was a large, attractive-looking book which contained many photographs of the shrine. Together with other photographs which we took ourselves, this book has become an excellent reminder to us of the places which we actually visited and touched.

Two months later, in October 1991, I was in Seoul, Korea, on a business trip. On one weekend, I took an express bus to Naju for the first time to see the Blessed Mother's weeping statue and to take a few photographs, if possible. Totally unexpectedly, this trip to Naju became the beginning of our work to promote the information about Naju in the English-speaking countries. In doing this work for the past ten years—publishing books, videos, newspapers, and brochures—we have felt a need for a photo album on Naju similar to the one we bought in Lourdes. It would serve both as a collection of long-lasting photographic reminders to those who actually visited Naju and as a general-but-vivid introduction of Naju to those who have not visited there yet. It could also be a nice companion for our other publications such as the message book, *Messages of Love,* and several videos which have already been produced.

There would be one important difference between the photo album on Lourdes and one on Naju, though. Lourdes is a fully-established shrine with several magnificent churches, many supplementary buildings, and vast gardens, while Naju is a shrine in its infancy. The main basilica, which the Blessed Mother has requested to be constructed on a mountain near Naju, will be built only after the Church officially announces that the messages and miraculous signs in Naju are of heavenly origin. We have no doubt that this official recognition will come. Until then, however, Naju is still going through persecutions, as in all the other shrines before it, by those who find it difficult to believe in the possibility of supernatural intervention by God in human history. We ask all those who love Our Lord and Our Lady to continue and increase their prayers so that this tremendous heavenly gift to the whole Church and human race will become an occasion for abundant eternal blessings for numerous people in the world as soon as possible.

Even though a new photo album on Naju cannot show the basilica and other supplementary structures yet (except the Chapel and the Blessed Mother's mountain), it can still contain many precious photographs of the numerous miraculous signs from God since 1985 when the Blessed Mother began to weep through her statue in Naju. Monsignor Matthias Perez Merino, a theologian in Rome, visited Naju in September 1990 and said that Naju was a synthesis of all the Marian messages and signs. Indeed, the messages received by Julia Kim of Naju from Our Lord and Our Lady are comprehensive and intense and do resonate with many of the messages given at other locations (which have Church recognition). The miraculous signs which have occurred in Naju—tears and tears of blood through the Blessed Mother's statue, fragrant oil, fragrance of roses, the Stigmata, mystical sufferings, miraculous changes of the Eucharist into visible Flesh and Blood, and miraculous descents of the Eucharist—have also occurred at different places in the world at different times in Church history. However, there has been no other place where all these signs occurred at one same location or through one same person. It seems that the intensification of the Blessed Mother's efforts to defeat the devil and open a new era for the glory of God, which began in Guadalupe, Mexico, in 1531, is approaching its climactic conclusion through Naju. In this context, a photo album on Naju could be a description of a critically important segment of Church history or its still-continuing unfolding, to which all of us have been called to make small-but-essential contributions. Hopefully, it may also serve as an instrument by which we become more deeply aware of God's boundless love and mercy for us and His ardent Will to save us despite our unworthiness.

May God bless you all!

Sang M. Lee
September 8, 2001
Nativity of Our Lady

Chronology

1784   Seung-Hoon Lee, a Korean scholar, visited Beijing, the capital of China, as a member of the official envoy of the Korean government and, during his stay in China, learned about the Catholic Faith. He became the first Korean baptized into the Catholic Church. After his return to Korea, the Faith spread rapidly, but was met with a fierce resistance by those who considered the new Faith a threat to their centuries-old Confucianist and indigenous traditions. For almost 100 years until the late 19th century, about 20,000 Korean Catholics, one Chinese priest and many French clergy were martyred. Pope John Paul II canonized 103 of them in 1983. Currently, there are about three million Catholics in South Korea (just over six percent of the population of forty seven million). More than twenty percent of the population is Protestant.

1947   Julia Kim (maiden name, Hong-Sun Yoon) was born in Naju, a small city in the southwestern tip of the Korean peninsula. Her father was a school teacher. Julia lost her father and grandfather in the Korean War (1950-53), and, together with her mother, began experiencing many hardships. She left junior high school to earn wages.

1972   Julia married Julio Man-Bok Kim. Julio has been working for the City of Naju in its agricultural department. They have four children— two sons and two daughers.

1980-1 Upon a miraculous healing of her serious illness after a meeting with a Catholic priest, Julia decided to convert to the Catholic Faith. She had belonged to a Presbyterian community. On Easter Sunday, 1981, Julia and her family were baptized at the Naju Parish Church.

        One night while she was praying, Julia saw a vision of Jesus suffering and bleeding on the Cross. She saw Our Lord's Sacred Heart torn apart by human sins. She promised the Lord to live a life of suffering in reparation for His wounds and for the conversion of sinners.

1985   Near midnight on June 30, while Julia was praying the rosary, the Blessed Mother's statue in her room began weeping for the first time. The next morning, the Pastor of Naju came to see this, followed by others. Soon there were thousands of people every day who came to see the Blessed Mother's weeping statue and to pray before it.

On July 18, Julia received the Blessed Mother's first message.

1986   On October 19, the Blessed Mother wept tears of blood for the first time.

1987   On January 14, Father Raymond Spies, a Salesian missionary priest from Belgium, became Julia's spiritual director.

On April 21, Julia suffered the pains of the Crucifixion.

On May 12, Julia suffered the pains of abortion.

On December 8, the Blessed Mother's statue was moved from Julia's apartment to the newly-built Chapel. Since then, the Blessed Mother's statue has been placed on the altar in the Chapel.

1988   On February 4, Julia suffered the pains of the Crucifixion and received the Stigmata.

On June 5, Julia smelled the odor of Blood from the Eucharist she received at the Naju Parish Church.

On July 29, Julia suffered the pains of abortion.

1989   On July 29, Julia suffered the pains of the Crucifixion and the pains of St. Andrew Kim's martyrdom. She received the Stigmata again.

1990   On January 13, Bishop Daniel Chi of the Wonju Diocese in Korea came to Naju. After a novena in the Chapel, he witnessed tears of blood flowing from the Blessed Mother's statue and left a written testimony: *I clearly saw and firmly believe.*

On March 25, Julia spoke at a Marian conference in Pittsburgh, Pennsylvania. About seven thousand people including several hundred priests enthusiastically heard the Blessed Mother's messages from Naju. She was also invited to the White House and spoke before President George Bush's advisors, urging them to work harder for the protection of human life.

On September 26, Monsignor Matthias Perez Merino, a theologian from the Vatican, came to Naju and said that Naju was a synthesis of all the Marian messages.

1991   A Eucharistic miracle occurred in the Naju Parish Church on May 16. During a Mass concelebrated by Fr. Jerry Orbos and Fr. Ernie Santos from the Philippines, the Sacred Host Julia received turned into visible Flesh and Blood in her mouth.

1992   On January 14, the Blessed Mother wept for the last time through her statue in Naju. She wept for a total of 700 days. According to Fr. Raymond Spies, this number signified intensity and perpetuity, as 700 is 7 times 10 times 10, a repeated emphasis. Fr. Spies said that, even though the external signs of the Blessed Mother's weeping in Naju ended, she actually weeps for us always and until the end of the world.

In May, Julio, Julia, and other pilgrims from Korea and the Philippines visited the Holy Land, Paris, Lourdes, Lanciano, and Rome. In St. Francis' Church in Lanciano and in their hotel room in Rome, Eucharistic miracles occurred again. While in Rome, Julia met the Holy Father and received his blessing.

On November 24, the Blessed Mother's statue in Naju began to exude fragrant oil. This miraculous sign continued for 700 consecutive days until October 23, 1994.

1993   In late October, Julia traveled to the USA to speak at several churches in Los Angeles and other cities.

1994   Another Eucharistic miracle occurred in the Naju Parish Church. The Mass was celebrated by Fr. Jerry Orbos from the Philippines, Sept. 24.

In late October, Julia was invited to speak in several churches in the United States and Canada.

On November 2, in St. Anthony's Church in Kailua, Hawaii, the Eucharist she received from Fr. Martin Lucia turned into visible flesh and blood.

On November 24, Archbishop Giovanni Bulaitis, the Apostolic Pro-Nuncio in Korea, visited the Chapel in Naju and witnessed two miraculous descents of the Eucharist. He also experienced an intense fragrance of roses. Afterwards, he made a detailed report to the Holy Father and several Cardinals in the Holy See.

In December, the Kwangju Archdiocese formed an investigating committee.

1995   On July 1, during an overnight prayer meeting in the Chapel, seven Sacred Hosts descended to the altar in front of the Blessed Mother's statue. The next day, by the order of the local Archbishop, the seven Sacred Hosts were consumed by two priests (Fr. Francis Su and Fr. Pete Marcial) and five lay people including Julia. The Eucharist received by Julia turned into visible Flesh and Blood in her mouth. A baby girl who was hopelessly ill with epilepsy was miraculously healed when Fr. Marcial blessed the baby with the Precious Blood from Julia's tongue. Later a sample of this Blood was subjected to a DNA test at a medical laboratory at Seoul National University and was found to be human blood.

On September 22, Bishop Roman Danylak came from Toronto, Canada, and witnessed a Eucharistic miracle during an outdoor Mass near Naju.

In October, Julia was invited to attend Mass celebrated by the Holy Father. During a Mass in the Vatican on October 31, a Eucharistic miracle through Julia occurred and was witnessed by the Holy Father. Two years later, in 1997, photographs of this miracle were allowed to be on display at Our Lady of Mercy Church in San Giovanni Rotondo, which is the shrine in honor of Blessed Padre Pio, together with photographs of other Eucharistic miracles in Church history which have already been officially recognized by the Church.

1996   During the overnight prayer meeting on July 1, several Sacred Hosts miraculously descended and entered Julia's mouth. She also received the Stigmata. The next day, she received the Stigmata again, and her hands were examined by two doctors in Kwangju, who wrote statements saying that there was no medical explanation for Julia's wounds.

On September 17, during a Mass concelebrated by Bishop Dominic Su and other priests in the Sacred Heart Cathedral in Sibu, Malaysia, the Sacred Host Julia received turned into visible flesh and blood in her mouth. In his letter to Archbishop Giovanni Bulaitis, the Apostolic Pro-Nuncio in Korea, dated November 8, 1996, Bishop Su stated that he considered the Eucharistic phenomenon he witnessed "a miracle."

On October 19, another Eucharistic miracle occurred through Julia during a Mass in the Naju Parish Church concelebrated by about thirty priests from different countries.

1997   In May, Julia visited Hong Kong and Macao spreading the messages.

On June 12, Bishop Paul Kim of the Cheju Diocese in Korea came to Naju and witnessed a miraculous descent of the Eucharist during a prayer in the Chapel.

On August 27, while Fr. Raymond Spies and Fr. Francis Elsinger from Hong Kong were visiting, there was again a miraculous descent of the Eucharist in the Chapel.

In November, Julia visited Los Angeles to speak in several churches.

1998   On January 1, Archbishop Victorinus Youn of Kwangju announced a declaration with a negative ruling on Naju. This has been followed by many questions inside and outside Korea on the doctrinal integrity and other aspects of the Kwangju Archbishop's declaration and calls for a re-investigation of Naju.

2001   During all the Korean bishops' *ad limina* visit to the Vatican, the Holy Father asked the Korean bishops about Naju, and Bishop Paul Kim of the Cheju Diocese made a detailed report to the Holy Father about the situation in Korea and asked His Holiness to open a new investigation by an international committee.

In the mean time, many pilgrims continue visiting Naju and messages continue spreading all over the world. Many miraculous spiritual and physical healings continue to occur. Graces from God through the Blessed Mother are intensifying in Naju.

Julia's Personal Testimony

The amazing Love of God saved me
from death and gave me a new life

As I look back at my past life, my mind becomes filled with amazement at God's Providence.

Early happiness taken away by the war

I was born 1947 in Naju, Korea, as the first child of the family. Until the age of four, my life had been a continuation of happiness. I was the darling child of the family.

Happy days ended when the Korean War broke out. My father and grandfather were killed by the Communists during the war, and soon my younger sister died also. My mother and I were the only survivors. We had to struggle with extreme poverty and other difficulties.

I had to drop out of junior high school because of financial difficulty, even though I was anxious to study more. In 1972, I married Julio Kim, who was the eldest among eight. We had four children—two boys and two girls.

Crisis in health

I was four months pregnant with my third baby. While I was doing housework, carrying my second baby on my back, there was some bleeding. I went to a gynecologist, who said that the baby in my womb was dead and that I needed surgery. I could not believe that the baby was dead. The doctor then asked my husband if he wanted me to live or die. I was tied to the surgery table and was operated on. It was the beginning of my sufferings.

I had a second surgery seven days later. One day after the second surgery, I was almost dead and was moved to a larger hospital. Three days later, I regained consciousness, but remained in serious condition. I tried many things to improve my health, but nothing helped. The gynecologist said that it might help if I had another baby. After much difficulty, I became pregnant.

Labor began in the ninth month of pregnancy, but the baby could not be delivered. The doctor suggested a Caesarean operation, but my mother-in-law

Julia (front right) with her teachers and friend in the sixth grade

Julia and Julio, her husband, with their first two children

insisted on a natural birth. To obey her, I continued suffering terrible pains for the next two months. My mother could not watch me in that condition any longer and brought some medicine from an Oriental herbal doctor. I took the medicine and delivered the baby in the eleventh month of pregnancy. I lost a large quantity of blood and became unconscious.

Two weeks later, my mother-in-law came and told me to go out and buy some rice. While I was returning home with the rice, I found myself bleeding again. Severe pains continued through the night, and my feet became swollen. I cried a lot when I was alone.

One day, when the baby was four months old, I was doing some laundry at a creek and suddenly found the baby being swept away by the creek. I plunged into the water and pulled the baby out. Soon, I developed a fever and severe pains in my belly. The doctor said that I had appendicitis and sent me to a larger hospital in Kwangju. Test results showed that I had inflammation in the pelvis, appendicitis, pregnancy outside the womb, and a fever. I seemed to be nearing death. I felt like going to the bathroom, but, instead, was taken to the operating room, and the surgery began.

For one week after the surgery, I vomited what I ate. I had trouble walking to the bathroom. Nurses complained that I was exaggerating and kicked me on my legs. After I came home, pains became worse.

About a month after the surgery, something was coming out together with blood and pus from where the surgery was done. Rosa, my eldest daughter, was crying loudly and screamed, *"Mommy! Your intestines! What should we do? Mommy! What should we do?"* We embraced each other and cried. We found out that it was the gauze that the doctors forgot to remove during the surgery.

I visited a country clinic every day. Blood and pus continued flowing out for three months. I went back to the larger hospital where the operation had been done. The doctors said that, because of the substantial inflammation, I needed another surgery. I refused, because I did not have money. I continued visiting the country clinic, and the pains continued.

The condition was worsening, and pains were becoming unbearable. I was hospitalized again, but it was too late. The doctor said, *"We did our best. Go home and eat delicious food."* He found a widespread cancer in my body. When he tried to show it to my husband, I was startled and stopped him. I thought I would rather die than show the cancer to my husband.

After hearing the death sentence at the hospital, I came home but did not give up. I did not want to dishearten my mother who had had only me to depend on since when she was twenty-seven. I struggled, but could not even stand or sit. The parts of my body which were touching the floor were hardening. My mother and husband took turns to massage me, but my body was becoming colder. The blood pressure was 50 over 40. I could not eat or drink. Because of problems in my veins, I could not even get I.V. injections.

Despite all that, I was still alive. Several women belonging to a Presbyterian community took me to their place of worship and brought me back home several times, even though I wanted to go to a Catholic church. One day two Presbyterian women visited me and consoled me. When they were leaving, they said to each other outside the room, *"What a pitiful woman! Life is precious, but she would be helping her family by dying."* I thought, *"That's right! Why didn't I think of that?"* I prepared cyanide and wrote seven letters—to my mother, husband, four children, and whoever might be my husband's next wife.

Light shines at long last

As I was thinking about my father and about to carry out the plan, my husband suddenly came home from work—earlier than usual—and said, *"Honey! Let's visit a Catholic church today."* So, we went to a Catholic church in Naju.

To the priest, I said, *"Father! If God really exists, He is too cruel. Why should I drink this bitter cup (death)? What did I do to deserve it?"* I thought it was not fair. I thought that I had lived a good life despite so many adversities. I had helped many beggars, I had not confronted those who had hurt me…

Then, the priest said, *"Ma'am, you are receiving graces through your body. Even I have not received such graces. Believe what I say."* When I heard these words from the priest, I believed and responded by saying, *"Amen."* At that moment, my body, which had been cold like a rock, was becoming warm, and I was sweating all over my body. The Holy Spirit was working in me. We decided to become Catholics and bought several items at the Parish gift shop. I placed a statue of the Blessed Mother and a rose on my clothes chest and lit a candlelight. I began to pray.

On the third day, I heard the voice of Jesus: **"Approach the Bible. The Bible is My living Word."** I opened the Bible immediately and was reading Luke 8:40-48. It was about a woman who had a hemorrhage for twelve years. She had the faith that if she touched the tassel on the Lord's cloak, she would be healed. When she touched Him and was healed immediately, Jesus said to her, *"Woman, your faith has saved you. Go in peace."* There also was the story about Jairus' daughter. The Lord told Jairus, *"Do not be afraid; just have faith, and your daughter will live."* Because Jairus believed Jesus, his daughter lived again. I believed that these words were for me also and, with a firm belief, responded with *"Amen!"* At that moment, I was completely cured of the cancer and all the accompanying illnesses.

I felt like running or even flying. I began going to the Catholic church and also opened a beauty parlor. I joined the charismatic movement and the Legio Marie. My life was filled with joy and love.

The Lord opens the gate of Heaven after my repentance

It was December of 1981. During an overnight prayer meeting, the leader said, *"Tonight someone will receive special graces."* I believed that it would be realized to me also. At about 3 a.m., the leader asked the people, *"What is it that you desire?"* Immediately, I prayed fervently, *"Lord, I want to grow spiritually. I want*

Julia's beauty parlor in Naju. In her home on the second floor, the Blessed Mother began weeping through her statue on June 30, 1985. Soon afterwards, Julia moved to an apartment. Then, in 1987, the Blessed Mother's statue was moved to a newly-built Chapel. Julia's family moved to a house next to the Chapel.

my spiritual growth." In response, the Lord showed me extremely surprising scenes. I was so surprised that I felt like my body was becoming paralyzed.

What the Lord showed me was a replay of everything that had happened in my life—I was beaten numerous times by an uncle while working in his home; I was working in a factory day and night daily without ever receiving pay; I was beaten up by several women who were doing business with me, because they did not want to return to me the money that I had invested in the business; I was mistreated many times, because my father was not alive; and many other happenings that I did not want to remember. I began crying bitterly, realizing that, humanly speaking, it would have been impossible for me to have lived thus far, but it was the Lord Who has kept me.

I also prayed for those who had inflicted pains on me: *"Lord, have mercy on those numerous people. They did what they did because of me. They were Your instruments for tempering me. Therefore, they are victims because of me."* I could not help crying wildly, because I realized that they suffered harms because of me. *"Lord! Forgive this sinner. Forgive this sinner…"* I kept asking for forgiveness.

While I was deeply repenting and asking for forgiveness, the gate of Heaven suddenly opened and a bright light poured down upon me. I also heard the following words three times: ***"The gate of Heaven is open."*** I became a very little, lowly person and prayed anxiously, *"Lord, open my heart further. Open it more."*

Until then, I had thought that I had lived a good life and had never made any mistake. Such pride was replaced by a deep realization that I was the greatest sinner. My body hardened again. I came home, supported by others. While lying down, I prayed, *"Lord, whether I live or die, I leave it to You."* I offered myself up to the Lord.

The Lord's call to a mission

Three days later, I heard the Lord's voice again: ***"Daughter! God has worked in His servant's heart. Get up hurriedly! I will make Myself known through you, who are unworthy."***

When I heard these words, I was so surprised that I stood up right away. I knew that I was healthy again. I felt like flying. The Lord resurrected three days after death. He raised me up on the third day of my illness and repentance. *"Yes, Lord! I am totally Yours. Use me according to Your Will."*

For the next three years, the Lord allowed me everything that I wanted—even those things that I had in my mind only briefly. At every moment, the Lord showed me that there was nothing that was impossible to God.

The Lord also let me see the inside of other people's minds and understand the nature of others' illnesses. Because of this, I felt unbearable pains. The Lord showed me that those who were doing the Lord's work and were thinking that they were close to Him were inflicting greater pains on Him and crucifying Him with bigger nails. I prayed hard for them.

When Jesus was entering Jerusalem riding a donkey, many people were welcoming Him placing palm leaves and their clothes in front of the donkey. What if the donkey thought that people were welcoming it instead of the Lord? What will happen to Jesus Who is riding the donkey, if the donkey jumps up and down with joy? Yes, while we work to make the Lord known, we can fail to be humble and think that we are the ones who are doing the work. Then, we will make the Lord fall on the ground. The thought that this can happen to me also sent a chill down my spine. When I was participating in the charismatic movement, many people liked me and made me stand in front of people. But now I wished that I could work in humility and hiding. I prayed, *"Lord, I saw enough. Please do not show me any more. If it can be of any use for the conversion of sinners who are crucifying the Lord, I will gladly live a life of suffering." "Lord!, I am so unworthy, but, if it can be of even the tiniest help to the Lord's Work, I will gladly offer up my sufferings."* So, I consecrated myself and my sufferings for the conversion of sinners.

Since that time, I have received extreme pains numerous times. Three years later, I was preparing for death again. While I was going to the Holy Hour prayer meeting in Kwangju, I prayed, *"Lord, I am Yours, if I die. I am Yours, if I live. Your Will be done."* During the prayer meeting, I was completely healed.

Since then, the Lord allowed me more sufferings and restored my health as needed. From June 30, 1985, the Lord gave us His Mother's tears and, later,

Julio and Julia Kim with their four children in the Chapel in Naju

Soon after the Blessed Mother's weeping began, Julia closed her beauty parlor because of the increasing crowds coming to see the statue. Her family moved to the Soogang Apartments (above). On December 8, 1987, the Blessed Mother's statue was moved to the newly-built Chapel, and Julia's family also moved to a new house next to the Chapel.

tears of blood through her statue in our home and, between November 24, 1992, and October 23, 1994, fragrant oil through the same statue. He also sent us many messages that are necessary to all of us.

The Lord also revealed visible changes in the Sacred Host and caused the descent of the Sacred Host in the Chapel in Naju on several occasions, because so many children do not accept that the Lord comes to us as our Food because of His Love for us. I, a sinner, only hope and pray that all will amend their lives according to the Blessed Mother's messages, come aboard Mary's Ark of Salvation, and be saved. What I want for myself is to live in hiding, looking after the deserted in the world. Glory be to the Lord alone!

Lord, my Light and my Savior! Love is beautiful and sweet, but also is sacrifice and sweat. To make a beautiful flower of love blossom, I want to love even the bitter cold of winter and offer up the pains that visit me without ceasing, imitating the martyrs. I wish to be a comforter for You like a grain of wheat that falls to the ground and dies to bear much fruit.

The Blessed Mother's Miraculous Signs in Naju, Korea

1985

Near midnight on June 30, 1985, while Julia was praying the Rosary in her room, the Blessed Mother began weeping tears through her statue. She also began giving messages on July 18. Her weeping tears and tears of blood lasted intermittently for a total of 700 days until January 14, 1992.

The Blessed Mother: *"I want you to be happy. A husband and wife are joined together so that they may lead a happy life. But my Son becomes brokenhearted when they hate each other and do not forgive each other. You must love one another. Who are your closest neighbors? How can you say that you love me and love the Lord when you cannot even love those in your family? Sanctify your family through love and harmony. This is what my Son Jesus thirsts for."* (July 18, 1985; photo on July 20)

The Blessed Mother: *"Come back to my Immaculate Heart… I called you today for a special purpose. Renounce your ego and abandon selfishness. I will be your shield. Even the arrows of fire thrown by the devils will not harm you. Pray much without worrying. I want you to stand on my side and become courageous guides in saving this world permeated with evil."* (October 20, 1986; photo on July 23, 1985)

1986

The Blessed Mother:

"The path that leads to my Son Jesus is a narrow and difficult one of the Cross. The human race can be saved by this path, but most do not come near it."

"Combine your forces. Pray without ceasing for the souls that are not turning away from the road that leads to their perdition."

(September 15, 1986)

The Blessed Mother began weeping tears of blood on October 19, 1986.

The Blessed Mother:

"As the Father, the Son and the Holy Spirit are One, you must all become one, too, and console me."

The Blessed Mother's face became so miserable with tears and blood, as she weeps for her children in the world who are mired in sins and are not repenting. (October 25, 1986)

1987

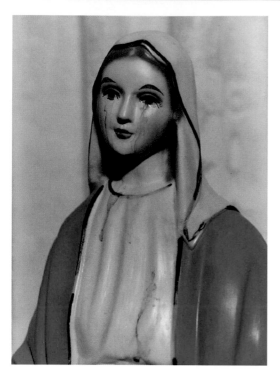

The Blessed Mother: *"My most beloved priests are now walking on the path of loneliness and a painful cross. They are climbing Mt. Calvary tired and suffering. They are walking on an alienated path of the cross, suffering many pains in their wounds. Help them. For the conversion of sinners who are deeply mired in evil habits and to follow the Will of my Son Jesus, priests are carrying the burden of teaching the way of love to the numerous souls who despise and ignore them countless times and the burden of offering sacrifices and reparations for those souls. I want you to pray with me for them so that they may not be infected by the world but may be faithful to their vocation. They are my sons who deserve respect and love by all." (April 23, 1987)*

Father Raymond Spies, Julia's spiritual director, came to Naju and witnessed the Blessed Mother's tears. (April 23, 1987)

The Blessed Mother: *"Every day, lower yourself further, thinking about Jesus on Mount Calvary. Through poverty, humility, obedience, and purity, keep going down from the high place to the low place following this Mother who wants you to walk the way of perfection. Shouldn't we become more humble like Jesus, Who chose to be humble? Change your life further—throwing away every attachment. Change your value system. Live a life of conversion. Convert every moment and converse with Jesus. Conversion does not just mean repenting sins. It means trying to live the life that God wants you to live. Abandon the worldly life and live a life based on the Gospels. Live like a lily. As the higher-grade protein gives rise to a more foul odor, the shiny things of the world entail a greater darkness. Let's die again and imitate Christ."* (June 14, 1987; photo on August 27)

On December 8, 1987, the Feast of Our Lady's Immaculate Conception, the Blessed Mother's statue was moved from Julia's apartment to the newly-built Chapel. Fr. Spies, other priests, and many lay people came to celebrate.

1988

On February 4, 1988, when Fr. Spies was visiting Naju, Julia suffered intense pains of the Crucifixion. When people committed sins, spears, arrows, and swords pierced her heart. After about twenty-five minutes of suffering, Fr. Spies felt so much pity that he blessed her, ending her pains.

1989

The Blessed Mother: *"A huge battle has begun like this already. Since it is a spiritual war, arm yourselves with me, by entrusting everything to my Immaculate Heart. Also, practice the messages of my love. Then, you will be able to escape from the terrible chastisement approaching the human race and the Church."* (August 26, 1989)

The Blessed Mother:

"Pray and offer sacrifices and reparations constantly for the Pope, Cardinals, bishops, and priests. Those who are being controlled by the devils are trying hard to strike down the Holy Father and lead the Church to destruction. But all the devils will lose power when my tears and blood are combined with your sacrifices and reparations."

(October 14, 1989)

From left: Rufino Park (the Chapel administrator), a Sister from Belgium, Fr. Spies, and Fr. Louis Bosmans of Québec, Canada, witnessing the Blessed Mother's tears of blood. (October 14, 1989)

The Blessed Mother: *"Display the power of love. My Heart is burning intensely because of the deafness and blindness of the children who do not love. Because they do not repent, thus sinking deeper into sins, my Heart is burning and burning so much that it bleeds. The blood becomes mixed with tears and flows out of my eyes. Even so, they do not accept my words, and, because of this, the anger of God is flaming up very vehemently."* (October 14, 1989)

The Blessed Mother:

"You will be saved if you do not ignore my tears and tears of blood, accept my words well, and live a life based on the Gospels. But, if you fail to do so, major calamities from the sky, on the ground, and in the seas will continue to happen. The world will experience all kinds of disasters. There will be moments of incredible distress in the near future. Therefore, do not think that these are accidental happenings. Be awake and pray."

(October 14, 1989; photo on October 15)

The Blessed Mother: *"Try to receive Jesus with a clean soul by making frequent Confessions, even when you only have venial sins. Jesus established the Sacrament of the Holy Eucharist to nurture us with His Body and Blood, to unite with us, and to resurrect our bodies after death. We must praise this amazing Sacrament, but many souls are becoming unclean by failing to make frequent Confessions." (June 15, 1987; photo on October 15, 1989)*

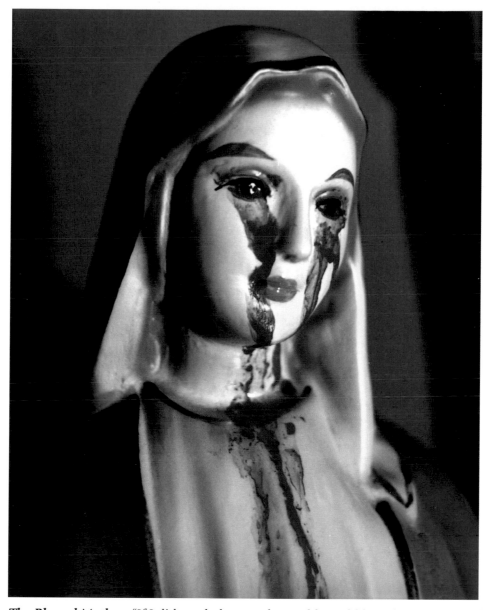

The Blessed Mother: *"If I did not help you, the world would have become seas of fire already. But I will never abandon you. Therefore, open your ears when you hear precious words and close your ears when you hear slanders. Even when you walk in darkness, follow me with confidence. Your sighs will turn into joys, if you accept my messages well and practice them." (October 14, 1989; photo on October 15)*

The western part of Naju as seen from a nearby mountain.
The arrow points to the Chapel.

On January 13, Bishop Daniel Chi of the Wonju Diocese in Korea came to Naju. After a novena in the Chapel, he witnessed tears of blood flowing from the Blessed Mother's statue and left a written testimony: "I clearly saw and firmly believe."

The Blessed Mother: *"The world will pass away, and so will all the passions. But you will surely be saved, if you hold the hands of this Mother, who is the string that ties heaven and earth together and who eagerly desires your salvation. You will live forever if you try to live according to the Will of God." (July 21, 1990; photo on May 3)*

The Blessed Mother:

"I am sad. So many of my poor children, who are usually forgetful of me, seek me only during hard times, as if trying to grab a life buoy… How can I work in such changeable hearts? Once they receive the grace they have asked for, they return to their miserable lives, forget about my love, and live in a despicable, ungrateful way. But, my daughter, my mercy prompts me to call them again. I am shedding tears of blood like this because of the poor children who are ungrateful for the blessings they have received, do not give love to others, and think that the graces they have received are their own and something they were going to receive anyhow for their own merit. Comfort my Immaculate Heart that is sufffering." (May 8, 1990)

The Blessed Mother:

"As my messages are spreading to the world and are being put into practice, the devils are becoming more and more active. The Red Dragon is employing all kinds of means to promote division, even among priests. Make our enemy, Satan, powerless with your faith and love. By doing so, help me save many souls. Offer to me even what you think are trivial things."

(May 8, 1990)

The Blessed Mother: *"My Son Jesus will bestow the cup of blessing on you through the loving benevolence of me, the string that ties Heaven and earth together." (May 8, 1990)*

The Blessed Mother: *"Many children are following me superficially by compromising with the corruptible flesh and the world permeated with errors. I am very sad, because there are only very few children who are following me truly with their hearts." (August 15, 1990; photo on October 2)*

The Blessed Mother: *"Many calamities are about to fall upon the world, but there are too many people who are self-centered. Those who love God and make me known will receive eternal life and will stand at the side of this Mother of Love. The world will change, but the Laws of God will not. Pray and pray again. Prayers of deep love are needed now more than ever for the Holy Catholic Church. This current age is extremely important for the whole human race." (October 4, 1990)*

The Blessed Mother:

"Come closer to me with love, entrusting everything to me. Spread my messages of love vigorously to all the children so that the lost Love of God may be restored in every corner of the world."

(October 4, 1990)

The Blessed Mother:

"There has never been another age when so many children of the world strayed so far away from repentance and brought ruin upon themselves in coopera-tion with the devils and under their control as now. All of them must listen to my voice of love. But, instead of listening to my earnest voice burning with love, they revolt against me…"

(August 15, 1990; photo on December 7)

1991

The Blessed Mother:

"Accept me warmly with prayers, sacrifices, reparations, and the offerings of consecrated hearts and sufferings. Thus, wipe away my tears and tears of blood shed for you by letting me live in your everyday life. By doing so, you will be preparing a place where Jesus, Who will be coming in glory, can reside."

(March 25, 1991; photo on April 2)

The Blessed Mother:

"You cannot win the victory without going through the cross. You must understand the amazing mystery of the Holy Eucharist by which God comes down from Heaven through priests in order to be with you. Therefore, make frequent Confessions to receive the Lord more worthily; open you heart widely, keep it clean and organized, and love one another so that it may become a palace and a tabernacle where the Lord can dwell."

(April 21; photo on April 2)

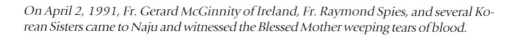

On April 2, 1991, Fr. Gerard McGinnity of Ireland, Fr. Raymond Spies, and several Korean Sisters came to Naju and witnessed the Blessed Mother weeping tears of blood.

At 6 p.m. on May 16, 1991, there was a Mass in the Naju Parish Church concelebrated by Fr. Jerry Orbos and Fr. Ernie Santos of the Philippines. Some parishioners of Naju and thirty-three pilgrims from the Philippines attended the Mass. At Communion, the Sacred Host Julia received turned into visible Flesh and Blood in her mouth.

Julia showing her tongue after she swallowed the Eucharist at the instruction of Fr. Orbos.

Witness to a Miracle

By Rebecca Ducusin
at Ave Maria Centre in Toronto, Canada

Father Jerry Orbos, SVD, knows that a miracle happens in every Mass, but when he gave communion to Korean visionary Julia Kim on three occasions and it turned into the visible body and blood of Christ, he asked for forgiveness for the many times he took communion for granted and came to a greater appreciation of the depth and privilege of being a priest.

The special message of the Eucharistic phenomena, Fr. Jerry Orbos, SVD, said, simply was to make us know the importance of Mass and communion. "We must pray the Mass. Jesus is really present there. We must feel Him. Don't rush the Mass, don't make it automatic."

Although he served in Korea as a mission priest for four years, he met the visionary Julia Kim when he went back to Korea for a pilgrimage from his native Philippines.

The 33 pilgrims led by Fr. Orbos witnessed the phenomenon on May 16, 1991, the second day of their pilgrimage, in the same church at Naju, Korea, where Julia had her first Eucharistic miracle on the feast of Corpus Christi in 1988 after receiving communion from a Korean priest.

Rufino Park, who gifted Julia with the statue of Our Lady that sheds tears and blood, approached Fr. Orbos, while he was cleaning the chalice after giving communion, to tell him that something was happening to Julia. Fr. Orbos approached Julia, who was kneeling down, trembling, and crying.

He said, "Remember she just received communion. When she opened her eyes she saw me and she opened her mouth. In her mouth was part flesh and part host. When I saw there was blood in her mouth, I was so shocked, scared, unworthy, but very happy. All I could do at that point was to say, 'Oh Lord, if this is what it is, thank you very much for the sign.' I prayed over Julia for discernment. And I prayed then, 'Lord forgive me, forgive us for the many times we took you so for granted in communion.' That was the whole thing. We take you so automatically. And for the times we take you so unworthily just for show."

After some moments, he asked the 33 Filipino pilgrims to see if something had happened. "The second time Julia opened her mouth we saw the blood,

Fr. Jerry Orbos (right) and other pilgrims praying with Julia after witnessing a Eucharistic miracle in the Naju Parish Church on May 16, 1991

but this time also on her tongue we saw the host that was still whitish and half of it was like flesh. When we saw that we were all crying, people were kneeling and then I just felt so much the presence of the Lord," a pilgrim said.

Fr. Orbos knelt before the tabernacle for a long time. Julia told Fr. Orbos that she saw, during the consecration, the Blessed Mother behind Fr. Orbos and Fr. Ernie Santos, spreading her mantle around them, embracing and protecting them in a very special way.

The late Salesian priest Fr. Ernie had kidney trouble but the pilgrimage rejuvenated him and he went back to East Timor where he worked hard propagating the faith.

In 1992, the second pilgrimage took them to the Holy Land, then to Lourdes and Rome. Julia was feeling well from Rome to Paris, Lourdes to Paris, but started to experience pain on the shuttle bus taking them to the plane. A pilgrim recalled seeing blue veins twitching on her face. The pain Julia felt was like those dealt by hammer blows on the head, a pilgrim recalled. She needed a separate room that evening.

The plan to have Mass at *Maria Majore* church the next morning was cancelled because of Julia's intense suffering and also Fr. Orbos' plan to visit the SVD house. Mass was celebrated in a room in Hotel Massimo so all 27 pilgrims could be together. During the Mass, Fr. Orbos told them that Julia, a victim soul, started to have pain the day before for the forgiveness of everyone. A pilgrim related what Fr. Orbos told them: "because while all of us in Lourdes decided to have cleansing of the body by going to the baths, and cleansing of the soul by going to confession, not all of us were truly repentant."

The Blessed Mother told Julia that she was being asked to suffer for them because they were not truly repentant. Julia was seated near the altar and was still in pain. Fr. Orbos gave the pilgrims a few moments to reflect and be truly sorry for their sins. Before the offertory, Julia coughed so violently that she was almost thrown out of her chair. Soon afterwards, she was smiling and expressed that everything was "OK" and the pain was gone because everyone was sorry for their sins. After communion, Julio, Julia's husband, called Fr. Orbos to show him that something extraordinary was happening. Everyone saw the host bleeding.

The next day, the pilgrims participated in a Mass at the *Miraculo Eucaristico* church in Lanciano where the first recorded Eucharistic miracle happened in the 8th century. They had prepared spiritually for the visit to the church as Julia herself announced, through an interpreter, that they spend the day in reflection. They did so by praying and singing.

As Fr. Orbos was returning the ciborium, he heard a commotion as people gathered around Julia. He became apprehensive. Seeing very vividly blood and the host turning into flesh and becoming thicker and thicker, Fr. Orbos called a parish priest of Lanciano to witness it and they both prayed over Julia.

After some time Fr. Orbos told Julia to swallow it. "Some people were saying get the specimen. I won't do that," Fr. Orbos explained. "She was to tell me later on that it was so hard to swallow it." "It was so hot," she said. "Fresh blood is hot," Fr. Orbos said.

On all three occasions when the host she received from Fr. Orbos turned into blood and flesh, Julia was asked to swallow it. Fr. Orbos always prayed for discernment.

After the Mass, Julia told Fr. Orbos that the vision she experienced during the consecration was that of Christ crucified and of a light coming from the Heart of Jesus going to the chalice, through Fr. Orbos and then extending to the people. Fr. Orbos said that he really felt so warm during the Mass. "Fine, good, thank you," he told Julia.

But the greatest surprise awaited them in the museum in Lanciano, where a large painting showed the vision Julia had during consecration.

Fr. Orbos' message is, "Stay close to Mary and you will never abandon Christ. You know, Mama Mary is very happy if we come close to her Son." He strongly urged that people form prayer groups and cenacles and devote some time to perpetual adoration. "The key is all here in our hearts."

"Mary is asking you to come closer to the sacraments, to the Eucharist. My only request now is please pray the Mass and make your communion more personal—feel the Lord. My dear friends, you don't have to see a Eucharistic miracle. Blessed are they who have not seen and yet believe. A miracle happens in every Mass." In leading the flock in praying the *Hail Mary*, he said, "we say it with all of our love" and when we come to the part 'pray for us sinners now,' we pause and pray what we want to ask."

"Regarding the Eucharistic phenomena which he was privileged to witness," he said, "I found that it was Mary who brought me closer to the Eucharist. We've studied all that in theology, but she allowed me to experience something which I could never forget. I am not saying that those are miracles. Let the Church take care of that." The Filipino priest added: "It has so stabilized my life, my priesthood, it is so clear."

"All of us have a vocation. Do your work well. Do your best. Life is short. We're all just passing by. Do something good and worthwhile. It so happened that God called me to be a priest to touch the lives of people."

Summer 1994

Inside the Naju Parish Church

On May 21, 1991, Fr. Spies and several pilgrims from Belgium visited Naju.

On June 8, 1991, an image looking like the Eucharist appeared under the sun.

Pilgrims looking at the appearance of the image of the Eucharist

On October 19, 1991, the Blessed Mother had tears of joy in her left eye. The Chapel was filled with an intense fragrance of roses throughout the overnight prayer meeting commemorating the fifth anniversary of her first tears of blood.

An image of the Eucharist appeared above the sun. The Chapel was filled with the fragrance of roses.

(November 27, 1991)

While Julia and others were on the mountain near Naju where the Blessed Mother requested a new Basilica, a powerful column of light appeared. (November 28, 1991)

Our Lady on Abortion

"My Heart is broken because of the unlimited birth control. Prevent abortions and pray for those who carry out abortions." (July 18, 1985)

"People are carrying out abortions even at this moment, causing intense pains in my womb. Pray the Rosary more fervently." (January 30, 1988)

"People are walking on the road toward Hell because they commit cruel murders and yet do not know that they are murderers. These little lives are deprived of their human dignity and receive terrible punishments that their parents deserve. Aren't these punishments too cruel for them?" (July 29, 1988)

"I am overcome with sorrow, because these innocent lives, precious lives given by God, are cruelly trampled, brutally kneaded, crushed, torn, and killed by ignorant and indifferent parents." (July 29, 1988)

"Tell everyone that a little baby is not a bloody lump, but has a life flowing in it from the moment of conception in the mother's womb." (July 29, 1988)

Fr. Jerry Orbos, Fr. Francis Su, Fr. Pete Marcial, and other pilgrims praying over Julia, who was suffering intense pains in reparation for the numerous abortions committed in the world. (July 1, 1995, during the overnight prayer meeting)

1992

On January 14, 1992, the Blessed Mother wept for the last time after a total 700 days of weeping tears and tears of blood since June 30, 1985. Julia mentioned that the tears the Blessed Mother had shed for the final several months were tears of joy.

Julia visiting Cardinal Jaime Sinn in Manila, the Philippines. (February 1992)

Stella Han, a Korean living in the Philippines and a Presbyterian, decided to convert to Catholicism after meeting Julia and working as her interpreter. She was baptized and confirmed by Cardinal Sinn. (February 1992)

Julio and Julia renewing their marriage vows in the church in Cana, Israel
(May 24, 1992)

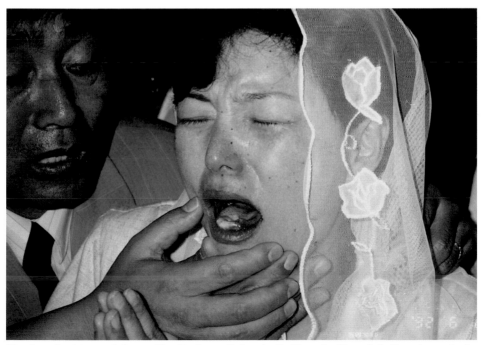

During the Mass celebrated by Fr. Jerry Orbos in St. Francis Church in Lanciano, Italy,
another Eucharistic miracle occurred through Julia. (June 2, 1992)

On June 3, 1992, a group of twenty-seven Filipino and Korean pilgrims, including Fr. Jerry Orbos, Julio, and Julia, visited the Holy Father and presented photographs of the Blessed Mother weeping tears of blood to His Holiness.

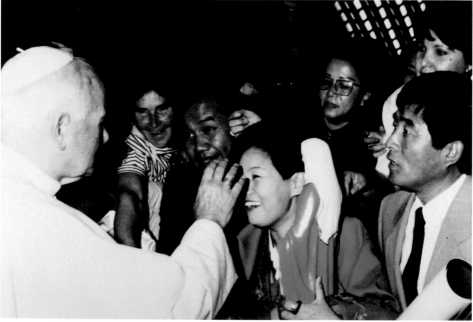

The Blessed Mother: *"Spread my messages of love courageously in every corner of the world. You will experience many difficulties, but do not forget that I am with you always." (May 31, 1992; photo on October 20)*

Two priests from the Philippines praying over pilgrims at the end of the overnight prayer meeting in the Chapel (October 20, 1992)

*Julia speaking to the pilgrims at the end of the overnight prayer meeting
(October 20, 1992)*

Father Aloysius Chang (standing), Rufino Park and Julia visiting Fr. Spies at his residence in Anyang, a small city south of Seoul (November 21, 1992)

On November 24, 1992, the Blessed Mother's statue began exuding fragrant oil while Fr. Spies was visiting. Fragrant oil continued flowing for the next 700 consecutive days until October 23, 1994.

1993

Fragrant oil flowing from the Blessed Mother's forehead
(April 7, 1993)

The Blessed Mother: *"What is the Last Supper? It is a feast of love and sharing. In order to give the totality of my love, which is so high, deep and wide, to my beloved Pope, Cardinals, Bishops, priests, religious and all my children in the world together with my Son Jesus, I am squeezing all of myself and giving you fragrance and oil. The fragrance and oil that I give to all are gifts from God. They represent my presence, love and friendship for you." (April 8, 1993; photo on April 7)*

Some of the photographs taken in April and May 1993 showed unexpected appearances of the Eucharist in the Blessed Mother's hands.

The Blessed Mother: *"Now the plans of my Immaculate Heart are about to be real-ized. Therefore, help the little unworthy soul (Julia) whom I have chosen, and make my wishes known to the whole world so that they may be put into practice. When the messages of love that my Son Jesus and I give you are realized in this world, the greatest victory of establishing the glorious Kingdom of Christ will be won, and you will see the glory at my side." (April 14, 1993)*

May 29, 1993

On May 27, 1993, Fr. Spies came to Naju. The Blessed Mother called him and Fr. Aloysius Chang to the mountain where the miraculous spring is located.

*Father Spies and Julia looking at the Blessed Mother's statue exuding fragrant oil
(May 27, 1993)*

*Father Spies drinking the water from the Blessed Mother's spring
(May 27, 1993)*

The Blessed Mother: *"My beloved daughter! Why do you hesitate at this hour when you should enter the battle? God's mercy will take root at this fertile place, which will be prepared with love, and accomplish miracles of love through you, my children. Therefore, hurriedly invite Fr. Spies and Fr. Chang, who have accepted my call, to the mountain chosen through you. Following the Will of God, Who gave you free will, I am going to make this place a shrine of mine and wash numerous souls that are walking toward hell." (May 27, 1993)*

On June 27, 1993, the Sunday celebrating the establishment of the Papacy, Julia was inspired to take several photographs of the Blessed Mother's statue. When the photos were developed, they showed clear images of the Sacred Host and a chalice, to everyone's surprise. In one of these photos, the Sacred Host had images of the Cross and the letters "A" and "Ω".

In another photo taken on the same day, there were images of the Sacred Host with five blood marks from Our Lord hanging on the Cross, and a chalice. In 2000, Dr. Tonsmann, an internationally recognized expert on the image of Our Lady of Guadalupe, examined this photograph and found an image of the Blessed Mother under the Cross.

This photo also shows images of the Eucharist with five blood marks and the chalice. At the foot of the Blessed Mother's statue are little pieces of cloth placed there to collect fragrant oil.

An enlargement of the image of the Sacred Host

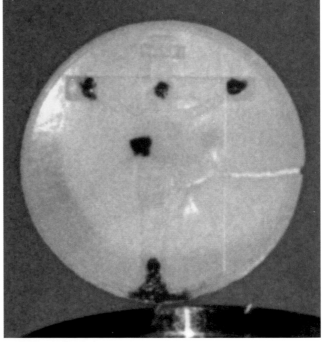

The Blessed Mother's Message on June 27, 1993

Daughter! My Son Jesus gave Peter the Keys of Heaven. Isn't the Pope the successor of Peter? Pray and offer sacrifices for the Pope. Support and protect him. As the Vicar of My Son Jesus, he is carrying a heavy cross. He has been consecrated to me, loves me so much and accepts me so well… He already understands my words that I am giving to all with tears and tears of blood in Korea.

To the Pope, who is my son, whom I love without limit and whom I can put in my eyes without hurting them, I will give a special love and sign.

So many children in the world are mired in the secular spirit. They continue committing sins, driving more nails on the Lord, pressing down the crown of thorns harder on His Head, and, thus, making Him shed more Blood. However, the Lord does not bleed in vain, but drops His Blood into a chalice and gives It to all His children through the priests whom He has called. But how many of the children are accepting Him?

The Lord saved you through His Passion and Death on the Cross. He saved all of you with His Precious Blood, Wounds, and painful Death and is leading you to the Life of Resurrection through His Body and Blood in the Blessed Sacrament. Now all priests must teach the importance of the Holy Eucharist to all the children in the world, as they celebrate the Sacred Mass with true love and sincere participation. Thus, today I make this request to my beloved son, the Pope.

I have manifested the images of the Holy Eucharist in various ways so that all my children may understand the importance of the Holy Eucharist. Hurriedly become blazing flames of love, reparation and adoration toward the Lord Who is in the Holy Eucharist.

I will always stay close to the Pope, help him, protect him from dangers, and be with him in the Heavenly Garden. If my words are well accepted and practiced, the chastisement which is to fall upon all of you will turn into a Second Pentecost and the Church will be renewed by the irresistible power of the Holy Spirit and Love.

Julia offers up rosaries to the Blessed Mother and prays. After a while, the rosaries become fragrant. The Blessed Mother gave Julia the following messages on October 23, 1986, and January 1, 1988:

"Pray the Rosary more and offer up more sacrifices for world peace and human salvation... as I told you before, the Rosary defeats the devils."

1994

In his homily during Mass at the Naju Parish Church on September 24, 1994, Fr. Jerry Orbos recounted his witnessing of the Eucharistic miracle on May 16, 1991, in the same church. He was not expecting that another Eucharistic miracle was about to occur during this Mass.

When Julia received Communion from Fr. Orbos and returned to her seat, the Sacred Host began turning into visible Flesh and Blood in her mouth.

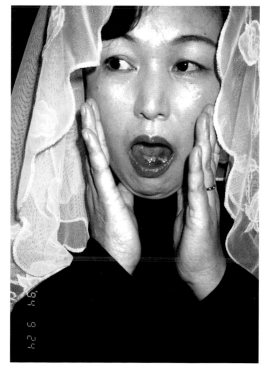

Father Orbos praying after witnessing the Eucharistic miracle on September 24, 1994.

The Blessed Mother:

"If all my children in this world transcend national boundaries, racial barriers and factional differences, form unity and harmony with each other, and display the power of love, the Church will be revitalized, a shining new Pentecost will be realized, and this world will be saved through the Lord, Who is present in the Eucharist."

Julia with the pilgrims from the Philippines after Mass on September 24, 1994

Julia's account of the Eucharistic miracle and a vision on September 24, 1994

Father Jerry Orbos from the Philippines celebrated Mass at the Naju Parish Church from about 11:40 a.m. About forty pilgrims from the Philippines, twenty from the U.S.A. and ten Koreans attended the Mass. During the Elevation of the Eucharist, I saw the merciful and smiling Jesus in the Sacred Host and felt an indescribable joy in my heart. I offered up an earnest prayer:

O, Lord! The King of Love, Our Savior, Who truly came to us by lowering Yourself to the extent of becoming our Food in order to save us! Have mercy on Your children so that they may repent hurriedly and be able to avoid the approaching calamity of fire.

After receiving Holy Communion, I came back to the pew and began meditation. At that moment, I clearly smelled Blood in my mouth and asked Rufino and Andrew sitting next to me to take a look. They were surprised and hastily informed the priest. Fr. Orbos and others gathered around me and some began crying loudly after witnessing what was happening. They saw the Sacred Host becoming yellowish brown from the edge and, then, thin blood veins appearing all over the Host. The blood was filling my mouth. After a while, Fr. Orbos told me to swallow the Host, which I did. Soon, I entered an ecstasy and saw a vision.

Numerous people were on board several large ships which were sailing in the ocean. I was in one of them. The ship I was on board was simpler than others, but had a large image of a dove at the head of the ship and, a little behind it, two banners. The banner on the right had an image of the Sacred Host and a Chalice and the other on the left had a large "M" on it. Between the two banners was Our Mother of Mercy wearing a blue mantle. She was so beautiful and filled with love. She was guiding the ship.

Other ships, on the other hand, had an image of the Red Dragon erected on board and were brightly and luxuriously decorated in different colors: red, green, yellow and so on. There were large crowds of people in those ships eating, drinking and noisily enjoying themselves. At that moment, several people in our ship looked at the people in other ships with envious eyes. Immediately, those in other ships noticed this and helped them cross over to their ships. The Blessed Mother implored them not to go, but they ignored her and left. The Blessed Mother was weeping silently and sadly.

Some time passed. A big storm was approaching and the sky was turning black. Soon, fireballs were falling from the sky. The Blessed Mother promptly stretched out her mantle and covered us. We were safe. But those in other ships were burning and screaming. They fell into the sea and drowned after some struggle. It was a terrible scene that one could not even look at with open eyes. The Blessed Mother was watching this shedding tears and with so much anxiety. She rescued several people who were approaching our ship, calling the Lord and asking for the Blessed Mother's help. They were people who had been blind and had fallen into the devil's deception, but repented and sought the Lord at the last moment. When the Blessed Mother finished rescuing them, the storm ended and the ocean became calm. The sky became clear and blue again, and a bright light was shining upon us. There were sounds of the angels singing: *Ave, Ave, Ave Maria…* At that moment, the Blessed Mother began speaking to all of us with a kind and gentle voice.

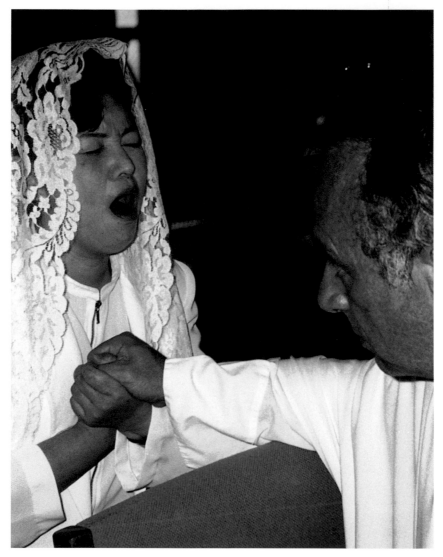

Father Martin Lucia witnessing a Eucharistic miracle through Julia in St. Anthony's Church in Kailua, Hawaii (November 2, 1994)

Jesus: *I wish to work miracles of love for all My children through the Eucharist because of My boundless Love for them, but they do not prepare themselves for receiving Me, do not realize My True Presence, insult Me with sacriligeous communions, and, thus, neglect and betray Me. Because of this, I am deserted by numerous children and left alone in the tabernacles, waiting anxiously for them to return to Me and give love to Me... Also have complete trust in and reliance on My Mother who is also your Heavenly Mother. My Mother, who is united to the sufferings of My Sacred Heart and is weeping tears and tears of blood and praying constantly so that all the children in this world may leave their sinful ways and return to My Bosom of Love, is the only one who can turn the just anger of God the Father away from you. (November 2, 1994)*

Father Lucia praying after witnessing the Eucharistic miracle

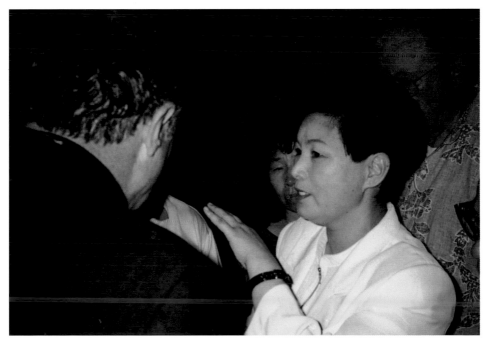

*Julia relaying to Fr. Lucia Our Lord's request that the importance
of the Holy Eucharist be made known more vigorously*

In her message on October 23, 1994, the last day of fragrant oil exuding from her statue, the Blessed Mother told Julia that she would call the Apostolic Pro-Nuncio to Naju. On November 24, 1994, Archbishop Giovanni Bulaitis came to Naju with his secretary (a Monsignor) and Fr. Spies. He came as the official representative of the Holy Father.

The Blessed Mother's message during the visit by the Apostolic Pro-Nuncio

My beloved daughter! I have a request to the representative of the Pope, my son, whom I love so dearly that I can put him in my eyes without hurting them. Ask him that a tabernacle be prepared beside me.

I feel so lonely, because many leaders are ignoring me for the sake of face-saving and the eyes of the world, paying no attention to my ardent request to look after numerous sheep that are walking toward hell...

So many priests are offering Mass unfaithfully. As a result, the Lord is unable to perform miracles of love in them through His Real Presence. He is suffering pains and is unceasingly calling the priests who are in sins to be faithful to their duties and become united with the Lord's Love.

Nowadays, errors are being taught even by some of my priests and are spreading all over the world. The Gospels are being promulgated by false prophets in such a way that the Gospels will become more acceptable to modern society under the pretext of civilization and innovation. But these are being promoted unfaithfully and are not the Gospels of my Son Jesus. While many kinds of sins multiply, they are being justified as if sewage water could be claimed to be pure water. Many blind people are believing such claims. The devil, who has led them into such deceptions, is overjoyed.

My beloved sons! Today I called you, whom I love most dearly, in a special way to this place where you will experience the Lord's Presence and mine as heroic and faithful witnesses so that the Mystery of the Holy Eucharist may be made known all over the world. So, help me hurriedly to save the sheep that have been lost.

I have said repeatedly that the Mystery of the Holy Eucharist, which is the Bread of Life from Heaven, is a spring that never dries and a medicine that gives you salvation. But only very few are making preparations before receiving Him. If my numerous children only knew that the Eucharist is truly the Life, the Everlasting Spring, the Manna and a perpetual miracle that is no less than the miracles of the Creation of the Universe and of the Redemption, they would not be walking toward hell...

The Holy Eucharist is the center of all the supernatural events, but is being trampled by so many children through sacrilege, insult and humiliation. Therefore, my messages of love must be spread all over the world more vigorously so that the time of the Lord, Who is present in the Eucharist, and of the New Pentecost may be advanced.

My beloved priests! When you spread my messages of love which I give you shedding tears and tears of love, you will experience pains, too. But I will elevate you, who have been called from all over the world, to a high level of sanctity so that you may reveal the true identity of the errors and promote the Truth with your mouths that will be like double-edged swords and thus may spread the fragrance of Christ. All the falsehoods, plots, tricks and cunning slanders will disappear in the presence of the light from God the Father, just as fog clears under the sun...

My beloved daughter! A certain priest living in sin was about to receive the Eucharist, but the Lord was not able to live in him and is having St. Michael the Archangel bring that Eucharist to my beloved Papal Representative and your spiritual director through you. So, stretch out your hands.

While Archbishop Bulaitis was praying together with others in front of the Blessed Mother's statue, Julia suddenly fell to the floor because of a powerful light from above. Then St. Michael the Archangel brought a large-sized Eucharist to her.

The Sacred Host was already broken into two
when Julia received It between her fingers.

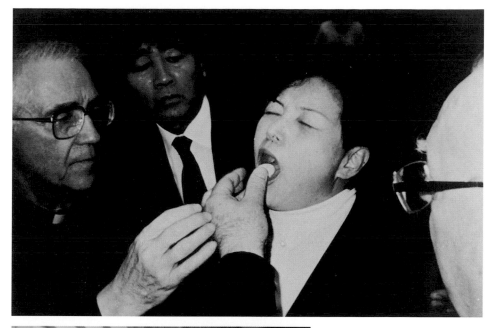

After Julia received the large Eucharist from St. Michael, the Blessed Mother asked her to hold hands with the Apostolic Pro-Nuncio and Fr. Spies. Suddenly, a small Eucharist came down and landed on Julia's tongue almost vertically. The Apostolic Pro-Nuncio took the Eucharist from her tongue.

Archbishop Bulaitis holds the small Eucharist which descended miraculously.
(November 24, 1994)

The Apostolic Pro-Nuncio explaining to other priests the miracles he just witnessed. The Chapel was filled with an intense fragrance of roses. (November 24, 1994)

The small Eucharist and a piece of the larger Eucharist that descended miraculously on November 24, 1994, being preserved in a monstrance in Fr. Spies' chapel in Gwachon, near Seoul. (1997)

1995

There was a Mass on June 30, 1995, at 7:30 p.m. in the Naju Parish Church concelebrated by the Pastor and seven priests from abroad. During Communion, the Eucharist Julia received turned into visible Flesh and Blood.

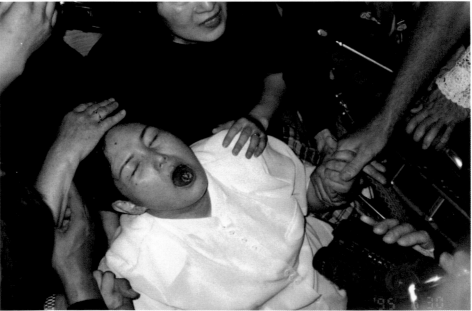

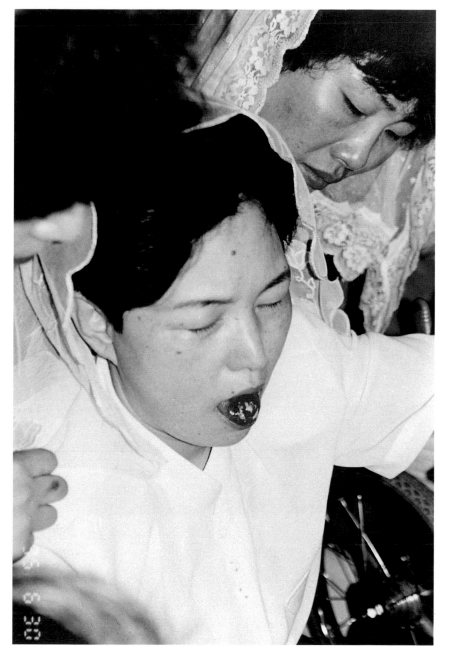

Jesus: *"If you have insulted Me by receiving Communion sacrilegiously, see the signs that I am giving you today and receive and worship Me with a most sincere heart. Then, I will heal your deep wounds, cure your illnesses and give you a gener- ous heart that can love everyone. I will give you the power to liberate yourselves from the powerful army of the devil, I will give you special graces that will be used as undefeatable and secure weapons, and I will give you a strong and tenacious power to practice goodness that can trigger a chain reaction more powerful than a nuclear reaction." (June 30, 1995)*

During the overnight prayer meeting on July 1, 1995, Julia saw Jesus on the wooden Crucifix above the Blessed Mother's statue turning into the live Jesus. Blood flowed from His forehead, His side, two hands, two feet, and Heart. Then the Blood turned into seven white Hosts and fell forcefully upon the altar before the Blessed Mother's statue. People in the Chapel heard sounds of the Hosts falling, like a hailstorm.

Jesus: *"This world has become one which is swarming with heretics. In this age which is placed in the middle of a danger, try to imitate Me. My real, personal and physical Presence in the Mystery of the Eucharist is an indisputable fact. I have repeatedly shown the Eucharist turning into visible Blood and Flesh so that all may believe that the Eucharist, which is a Mystery of the Infinite Love, Humility, Power and Wisdom, is My Living Presence. If certain priests do not believe in this Personal Presence of Mine in the Church, they certainly do not qualify as co-redeemers. When they ignore Me, Who is Christ, true God and true Man, they will be publicly denying My Divinity while acknowledging My human nature. That is because they have lost the ability to discern between good and evil and between authentic and unauthentic."* (July 1, 1995)

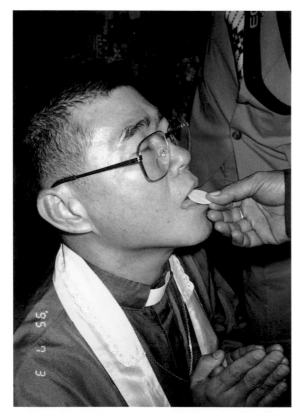

When the miraculous descent
of the seven Hosts was
reported to Archbishop
Victorinus Youn of Kwangju,
he sent the instruction
through the pastor of Naju to
have the seven Hosts
consumed as soon as possible.
In obedience, Fr. Francis Su,
Fr. Pete Marcial, and five lay
people including Julia
received these Hosts the next
day. Left: Fr. Su receiving the
first Host from Fr. Marcial
(July 2, 1995)

Father Francis Su prepares to give Communion to Fr. Marcial and five lay people.
(July 2, 1995)

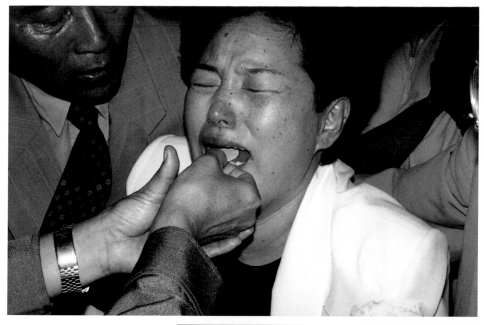

Above: Julia receiving the seventh Host from Fr. Su. She was crying because the seven Hosts could not be preserved.

Right: Shortly after she received Communion, the Eucharist in her mouth began turning into visible Flesh and Blood. Father Su and Fr. Marcial dipped their fingers in the Precious Blood on Julia's tongue and wiped them on a white cloth. When Fr. Marcial blessed with his finger a six-month old baby girl seriously ill with epilepsy, she was immediately healed. (July 2, 1995)

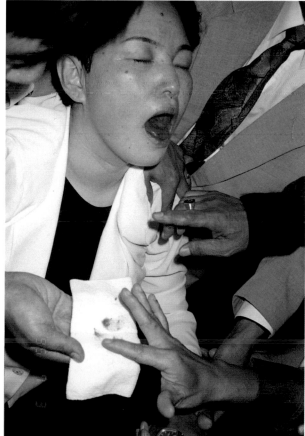

*Father Su displays the cloth stained with the Precious Blood
from the Eucharist in Julia's mouth. (July 2, 1995)*

*Pilgrims who witnessed the miraculous change of the Eucharist
into visible Flesh and Blood in Julia's mouth on July 2*

On September 22, 1995, during an open-air Mass on a mountain near Naju, concelebrated by Bishop Roman Danylak and Fr. Joseph Finn from Canada, and Fr. Aloysius Chang of the Archdiocese of Kwangju, a Eucharistic miracle occurred involving the change of the Eucharist into Flesh and Blood in the shape of small Heart.

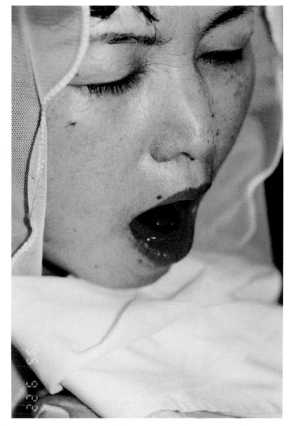

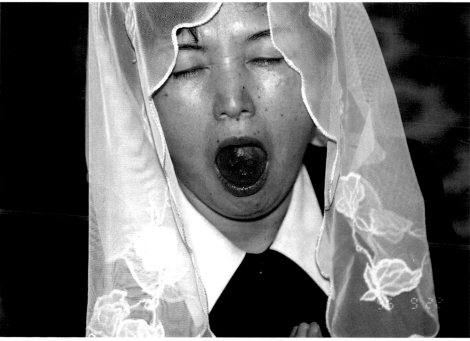

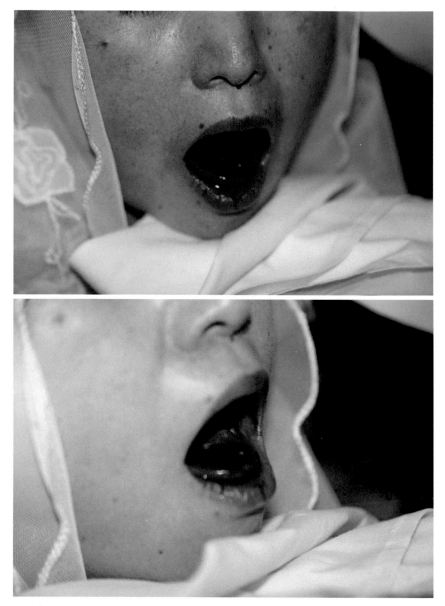

Jesus: *"If my priests, who celebrate Mass everyday, truly believe and feel My Real Presence and live the sublime and amazing Divine Reality, numerous souls will be purified and live in the grace from My merciful Heart beyond expectations through this Real Presence of Mine. Make My Physical Presence known hurriedly. This world is now on the brink of destruction because of human degradation, apostasy and infidelity, but too many of my ministers are asleep. Thus, even my ministers are being misled by false prophets. The present disorders are tormenting Me and keep tearing apart My Heart. This also becomes a whip and keeps tearing apart My Mother's Immaculate Heart… Because My Mother's loving and kind words for the past several centuries have been ignored, sin has reached a saturation point, even within the Church."* (September 22, 1995)

Bishop Roman Danylak and other witnesses of the Eucharistic miracle
on September 22, 1995

Bishop Danylak concelebrating Mass at St. Catherine of Siena Church in the Los Angeles
area in November 1997. He has been giving testimony to the Eucharistic miracle he wit-
nessed at many places around the world. Fr. Joseph Finn also published a book,
The Reality of the Living Presence, *as his testimony.*

Sworn Testimony of Bishop Roman Danylak to the Eucharistic Miracle in Naju on September 22, 1995

I, Bishop Roman Danylak, Apostolic Administrator of the Eparchy of Toronto for Ukrainian Catholics in Toronto, Canada, and titular bishop of Nyssa, herewith solemnly testify that I concelebrated the Divine Liturgy or Holy Mass, with the Reverend Fathers Aloysius Chang, parish priest of the Kwangju Archdiocese in Korea, invited by me to assist during my visit to Korea, and Joseph Peter Finn, retired priest of the London Diocese in Ontario on Friday, September 22, 1995, at 5 p.m. in an open-air celebration on the grounds of the valley where a future church is to be erected, God-willing, to the honour of the Blessed Virgin Mary and Mother of God.

Following the Liturgy of the Word, I delivered a brief homily for the occasion. After the communion of the priests, Fr. Chang and I administered Holy Eucharist under both species to Julia Kim and the eleven others. As we continued to distribute Holy Communion to the others present, we heard the sudden sobbing of one of the women assisting at Mass. The Sacred Host received by Julia Kim was changed to living flesh and blood. Fr. Joseph Finn, who had remained at the altar during the communion of the faithful, was observing Julia; he noted that at the moment he turned to observe Julia, he saw the white edge of the host disappearing, and changing into the substance of living flesh.

Fr. Chang and I returned to Julia. The Host had changed to dark red, living flesh and blood was flowing from it. After Mass, Julia shared with us that she experienced the Divine Flesh as a thick consistency and a copious flowing of blood, more so than on the occasion of previous miracles of the changing of the host into bleeding flesh. We remained in silence and prayer; all present had the opportunity of viewing and venerating the miraculous Host. After some moments I asked Julia to swallow and consume the Host. And after the Mass Julia explained that the Host had become large and fleshy; and that she consumed it with some difficulty. The taste of blood remained in her mouth for some time. I then asked that she be given a glass of water, from the miraculous source of water nearby. As she drank the water, her finger touched her lips, and a trace of blood was visible on her finger. She rinsed her finger in the water and drank it.

In testimony of this, I append my signature, together with the signatures of all the witnesses present.

Dated at Naju, this twenty-second day of September, 1995.
✠ **Roman Danylak, titular Bishop of Nyssa, Apostolic Administrator, Eparchy of Toronto, Canada.**
Joseph P. Finn, St. Peter's Cathedral Basilica, London, Ontario, Canada, et al. (Korean signatures of others present)

An image of the Eucharist appeared above the sun.
Seen from the Blessed Mother's mountain near Naju. (October 12, 1995)

One of the unusual sun phenomena in Naju (October 19, 1995)

Pilgrims from the USA afer breakfast at Shinan Beach Hotel in Mokpo, about an hour's drive from Naju. (October 21, 1995)

Pilgrims from the USA with Fr. Francis Su and Julia on the Blessed Mother's mountain where the miraculous spring is located. (October 22, 1995)

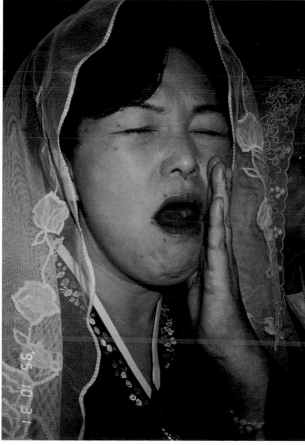

On October 31, 1995, at the invitation by the Holy See, Julia and Julio attended the Mass celebrated by the Holy Father in his chapel. When the Eucharist Julia received changed into visible Flesh and Blood, the Holy Father's secretary asked her to wait in the back of the chapel until the end of the Mass. In the above photo, Julia can be seen kneeling in the back while the Holy Father meditates.

Julia kissing the Holy Father's hand after Mass. Then she opened her mouth to show the Sacred Host to the Holy Father. (October 31, 1995)

The Holy Father witnessing the Eucharistic miracle (October 31, 1995)

The Holy Father giving rosaries to Julia and Julio (October 31, 1995)

After the Mass and audience with the Holy Father. From left: Julio, daughter Rosa, Monsignor Paik (Secretary General of the Korean Bishops' Conference), Julia, Monsignor Vincent Thu (personal secretary of the Holy Father), Raphael Song (interpreter), and Rufino Park (administrator of the Chapel in Naju). (October 31, 1995)

At the entrance to the Basilica of St. Michael the Archangel, below the Church of Our Lady of Grace in San Giovanni Rotondo, Italy, where Blessed Padre Pio lived. Inside is a display of various Eucharistic Miracles throughout Church History that have been officially recognized. The Eucharistic Miracle through Julia in the Vatican on October 31, 1995, was included in this display in May 2001.

MIRACOLO EUCARISTICO

in Santa Sede - Roma: 1995
natura: S. Ostia sulla lingua si converte in
carne e sangue

Questo mirabile miracolo Eucaristico il Signore lo ha manifestato davanti agli occhi di Giovanni Paolo II, anzi è uno dei protagonisti del prodigio soprannaturale. Il 31 ottobre del 1995 il Pontefice celebra la S. Messa, delle ore 7:30, nella cappella privata. Sono presenti, su invito, alcuni pellegrini tra i quali mons. Pak Dionysio, segretario della conferenza episcopale della Corea del sud, il seminarista Song Raphael e Julia Youn, il marito e due figli, sempre della Corea del sud.
Questa Julia è la mistica di Naju, dove in una cappella riceve messaggi della Vergine Maria, di cui lo stesso Pontefice ha mostrato interesse. Altri presenti sono: padre Raymond Spies, belga e padre spirituale di Julia e mons. (vietnamita) segretario privato del S. Padre. Alla Comunione, Julia ricevuto l'Ostia dalle mani del Pontefice, non riesce ad inghiottirla gonfiarsi e di sapore di sangue. Allora apre la bocca a mons. Pak, che il quale nota che l'Ostia si è convertita in carne e sangue vivo. Giovanni II, per nulla sorpreso ma meravigliato, osserva il prodigio e poi, amorevolmente benedice la mistica.
Il prodigio Eucaristico, benché fece eco tra i presenti, fu mantenuto secreto per circa due anni, ciò per evitare clamori un pò sensazionalistici.

Julia mostra il prodigio Eucaristico

Giovanni Paolo II lo ammira

la meraviglia del S. Padre

il Pontefice le tende le mani

I partecipanti alla S. Messa:

Panel in the display in St. Michael's Basilica describing the Eucharistic Miracle through Julia in the Vatican on October 31, 1995 (English translation of Italian text on next page)

Text of display in San Giovanni Rotondo
(English translation)

EUCHARISTIC MIRACLE

in the Holy See—Rome: 1995
Nature: Sacred Host on the tongue is converted into flesh and blood

The Lord manifested this marvelous Eucharistic miracle before the eyes of John Paul II, or rather, he was one of the main participants of the supernatural phenomenon. On October 31, 1995, the Pontiff celebrated Holy Mass at 7:30 a.m. in his private chapel. Those present, by invitation, were some pilgrims, among whom were Msgr. Dionysio Paik, Secretary of the Bishops' Conference of South Korea; the seminarian Raphael Song; and Julia Youn, her husband, and daughter, all of South Korea.

This Julia is the mystic of Naju, where in a chapel she receives messages from the Virgin Mary, in which the Pontiff has shown interest. Also present was Msgr. Vincent Thu (Vietnamese), private secretary of the Holy Father. During Communion, Julia received the Host from the hands of the Pontiff, did not succeed in swallowing it, for It began to swell and to taste of blood. Then she opened her mouth to Msgr. Paik, who noted that the Host was converted into live flesh and blood. John Paul II was not at all startled, but marveled and observed the phenomenon and then lovingly blessed the mystic.

The Eucharistic phenomenon, although echoed among those present, was kept secret for around two years, so as to avoid any sensationalistic clamors.

Photo captions:

Top left: Julia shows the Eucharistic miracle
Top right: John Paul II admires it
Second right: The astonishment of the Holy Father
Third right: The Pontiff extends his hands
Bottom left: The participants of the Holy Mass: Julia is behind the Holy Father
Bottom right: The Pontiff's blessing

1996

During the overnight prayer meeting in the Chapel on July 1, 1996, at about 3 a.m., Julia saw the Precious Blood dripping from the Seven Wounds of Jesus: head, Heart, both hands, both feet, and side. At the same time, a powerful light radiated from the wounds. Then Jesus' Blood turned into white Eucharists. As the light penetrated the same seven places on Julia, she screamed loudly out of pain and fell back. While her mouth was opened from screaming, the seven Sacred Hosts descended and entered it.

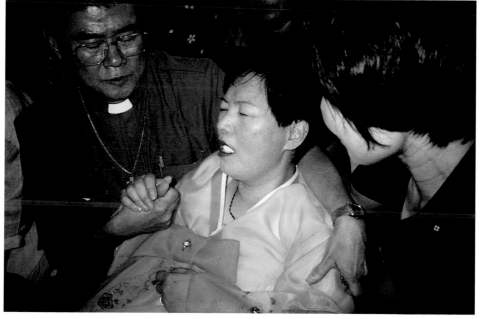

Father Spies, Fr. Su, and Rufino Park observe the Stigmata on Julia's hands.
(July 1, 1996)

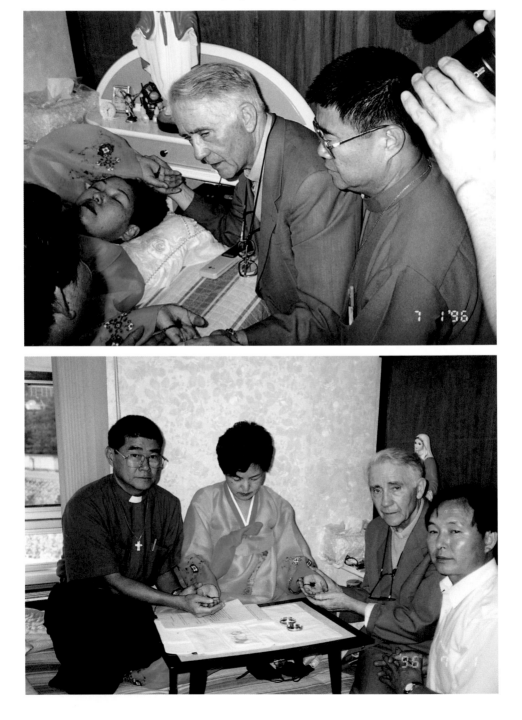

The next day, July 2, 1996, at about 1 p.m., while Julia was praying in the Chapel together with Fr. Spies and other pilgrims, light from the Crucifix again penetrated Julia's hands. She fell down to the floor and received a message from the Blessed Mother.

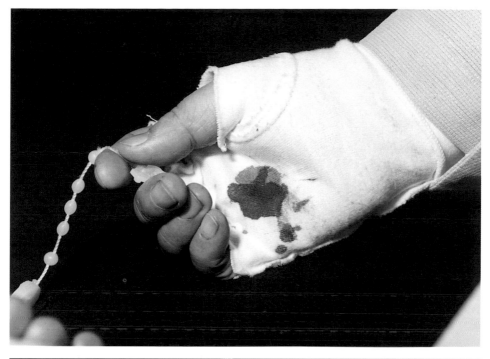

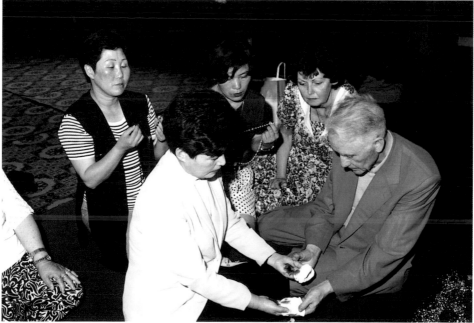

At Fr. Spies' instruction, Julia visited two hospitals in Kwangju and had her pierced hands examined. The doctors stated in writing that her wounds had no medical explanation. (July 2, 1996)

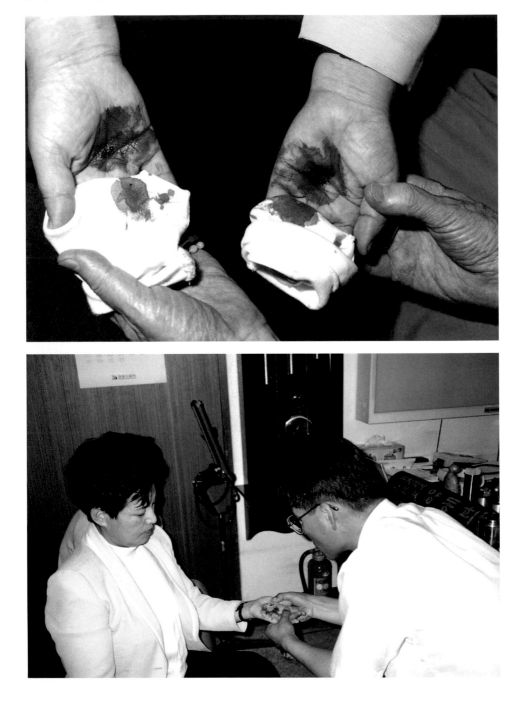

In September 1996, Julia was invited to visit the Diocese of Sibu, Malaysia, to which Fr. Francis Su belongs. In the evening of September 17, his brother, Bishop Dominic Su, was the main celebrant of Mass in Sacred Heart Cathedral in Sibu. The cathedral was packed with about three thousand people. During Mass, Bishop Su delivered a powerful homily on the importance of the Holy Eucharist. To everyone's surprise, another Eucharistic Miracle occurred through Julia during this Mass.

A choir of teenagers singing during the Mass
(September 17, 1996)

Father Francis Su with Julia during the Eucharistic Miracle
(September 17, 1996)

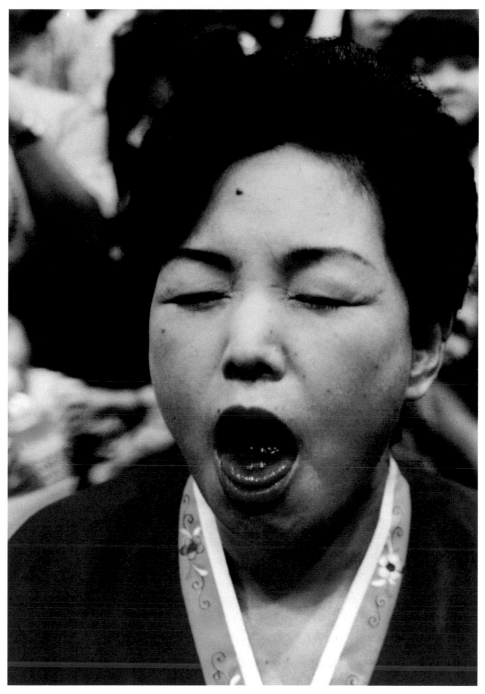

The Sacred Host changed into live Flesh and Blood in the shape of a small heart.
(September 17, 1996)

NUNTIATURA APOSTOLICA
IN COREA

Seoul, 1 November 1996

Your Excellency,

It has come to my knowledge the wonderful manifestation of the Holy Eucharist which took place in your presence last September.

This Nunciature is gathering material relating to events involving Julia and I should be most grateful if you could share with me the experience with a documentation, witness reports and photographs.

As you may know, I myself assisted at a marvelous presence of the Eucharist in November 1994.

I express my anticipated thanks.

Cordially yours in Our Lord,

+ Giovanni Bulaitis
Apostolic Pro-Nuncio

—————————————————

His Excellency
Most Reverend DOMINIC SU HAW CHIÙ
Bishop of Sibu
P.O. Box 495
96007 SIBU, Sarawak
MALAYSIA

BISHOP'S OFFICE,
P. O. Box 495
96007 Sibu, Sarawak, Malaysia.
Tel: No. 084-317373

8th November, 1996.

Most Rev. Giovanni Bulaitis,
Apostolic Pro-Nuncio,
Kwang Hwa Moon P.O.Box 393,
110-603 Seoul, Korea.

Your Excellency,

Thank you for your letter, dated 1st November, 1996.

I was caught totally unprepared when this extraordinary Eucharistic phenomenon occurred in our Sacred Heart Cathedral, Sibu on 17th September, 1996 during our Eucharistic celebration from 7.30 p.m. to 9.30 p.m.
When I think over it now, I can see that it was good for me to be caught unprepared. Had I expected beforehand that this mysterious incident would happen, I would have got a pyx ready to get this "flesh" and "blood" from the mouth of Mrs. Julia Kim for laboratory analysis. This would show that my faith in the real presence of Jesus in the Eucharist would have to depend on scientific proof. What Jesus wants from us is our child-like faith in Him and not an intellectual type of faith based on science and reasonings. That is why some Catholics, including a few priests, no longer believe in the real presence of Jesus in the Eucharist.

When our Lord Jesus performed His miracles in the very eyes of those Scribes and Pharisees, they refused to believe in Him. They called upon the Doctors of the Law, the Biblical scholars, theologians, etc. to assess Jesus. As a consequence of their assessment, they regarded Jesus as a sinner because He broke the sabbath law. They also accused Him of using the power of beelzebul to cast out demons. Eventually they succeeded to condemn Jesus to death.

I fully support our Church's stand on being very cautious to consider any "apparition" or "miracle" as genuine without first giving it a thorough investigation in order to avoid being led astray by any hallucination, deceptive forces, unhealthy element, etc. etc.
On the other hand we should also keep in mind the advice given by Gamaliel to his Council. "If what they have planned and done is of human origin, it will disappear, but if it comes from God, you cannot possibly defeat them. You could find yourselves fighting against God" (Acts 5:38-39).

(continued...)

There was no report being made in any public press about this incident that happened here on 17th September, 1996. Only those who were present at the Eucharistic celebration knew about it.

Those who believe in the real presence of Jesus in the Eucharist need no scientific proof. Those who do not believe, it does not matter what sort of scientific proof they get, they will still not believe.

During the time of our Lord Jesus, many simple and uneducated people believed in Him. Those few Scribes and Pharisees personally witnessed Jesus working miracles, healing the sick, raising the dead to life, feeding 5000 people with a few loaves of bread and fish, claiming to be equal to God and so no, they still did not want to believe in Him.

There is no point for me to make any publicity about this extraordinary Eucharistic manifestation. Those simple people with child-like faith believe it. Those sophisticated people with intellectual faith do not. Why waste time to convince them ?

The Holy See has to depend on the Bishop of Kwanju diocese - being the spiritual leader of his local Church - to assess whether those extraordinary Eucharistic phenomena happening in Naju were genuine or not since Naju is in Kwanju diocese. I understand that the whole thing there is now under cannonical investigation.

What happened in Sibu on 17th September, 1996 has nothing to do with the Bishop of Kwanju. It is the jurisdiction of the Bishop of Sibu to see to the matter. It has always been my belief in the real presence of Jesus in the Eucharist. I do not need any scientific proof to convince me.
I often encourage our people to turn to the Eucharistic Lord for help.

In my humble opinion and judgment, I would consider this extraordinary Eucharistic phenomenon as an Eucharistic "miracle". I enclose here 3 photoes which were taken during the incident.

Let the Name of Lord Jesus be praised forever and ever!

Yours respectfully in Christ,

.... *Jroff* ..

+ Dominic Su
Bishop of Sibu.

c.c. The Apostolic Delegate to Malaysia.
     The President of the Bishops' Conference of Malaysia, Singapore & Brunei.

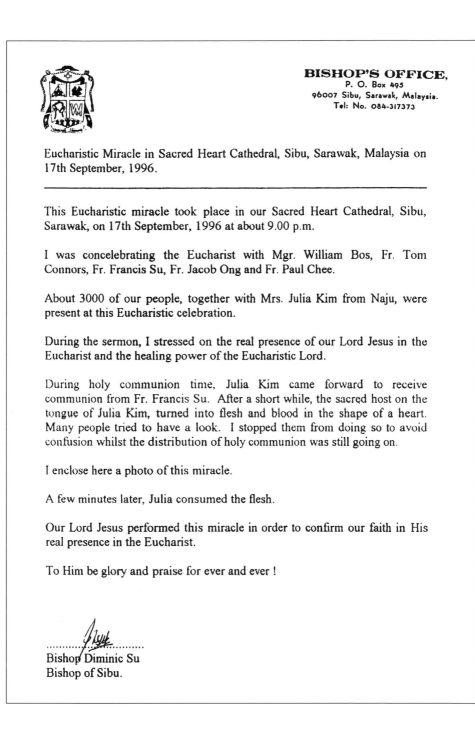

BISHOP'S OFFICE,
P. O. Box 495
96007 Sibu, Sarawak, Malaysia.
Tel: No. 084-317373

Eucharistic Miracle in Sacred Heart Cathedral, Sibu, Sarawak, Malaysia on 17th September, 1996.

This Eucharistic miracle took place in our Sacred Heart Cathedral, Sibu, Sarawak, on 17th September, 1996 at about 9.00 p.m.

I was concelebrating the Eucharist with Mgr. William Bos, Fr. Tom Connors, Fr. Francis Su, Fr. Jacob Ong and Fr. Paul Chee.

About 3000 of our people, together with Mrs. Julia Kim from Naju, were present at this Eucharistic celebration.

During the sermon, I stressed on the real presence of our Lord Jesus in the Eucharist and the healing power of the Eucharistic Lord.

During holy communion time, Julia Kim came forward to receive communion from Fr. Francis Su. After a short while, the sacred host on the tongue of Julia Kim, turned into flesh and blood in the shape of a heart. Many people tried to have a look. I stopped them from doing so to avoid confusion whilst the distribution of holy communion was still going on.

I enclose here a photo of this miracle.

A few minutes later, Julia consumed the flesh.

Our Lord Jesus performed this miracle in order to confirm our faith in His real presence in the Eucharist.

To Him be glory and praise for ever and ever !

....
Bishop Diminic Su
Bishop of Sibu.

Priests from various countries concelebrating Mass in the Naju Parish Church on October 19, 1996, commemorating the tenth anniversary of the Blessed Mother's first weeping tears of blood in Naju.

During this Mass, another Eucharistic miracle occurred. Father Spies examines the Sacred Host in Julia's mouth that has turned into visible Flesh and Blood. (October 19, 1996)

After the Mass at the Naju Parish Church, pilgrims gathered in the Naju Gymnasium for an overnight prayer service. (October 19, 1996)

Many priests also participated in the overnight prayer service. (October 19, 1996)

During a break. Father Spies sitting at the organ. In back, from left: Fr. Aloysius Chang, Julia, Julio, and Rufino Park. The statue of Our Lady was brought from the Chapel to the prayer meeting. (October 19, 1996)

Pilgrims collecting water from the miraculous spring on the Blessed Mother's mountain near Naju (October 20, 1996)

Pilgrims with Julia in the Chapel before their departure from Naju
(October 22, 1996)

Julia presenting a replica statue of Our Lady of Naju to Fr. Llamas of Venezuela (October 22, 1996)

Our Lord's Message on October 19, 1996

I am the Bread that came down from Heaven. I have repeatedly emphasized to you with signs that, if all of you open your hearts widely and accept Me, My Life and My Love will overflow to all of you. But My Heart is so distressed that It is bleeding, because only very few of the children are truly accepting Me. I showed a sign again today so that my children from various places in the world may believe in My Real Presence and spread It. Therefore, hurriedly let the importance of the Holy Eucharist be known in this urgent time. My Love prompted Me to want to be united with you by drawing all of My Life from My Essence Itself. If you, whom I love so dearly, do not accept this profound Love, what can I do? My Sacred Heart is burning vigorously, because I wish to save you with My Body, My Blood, My Soul and My Divinity, but there only are very few children who open their hearts widely and come near Me.

As I first took My Body in the womb of Mary, My Holy Mother, My Heart began beating for you in unison with hers. Therefore, love Mary, My Mother, and follow her words. You must know that loving and following her is loving and following Me.

1997

On March 20, 1997, the First Lady of Honduras visited Naju.

Julio and Julia Kim
(March 20, 1997)

In May 1997, Julia visited St. Anthony's Church in Macao. In this church, a replica statue of Our Lady of Naju and a statue of St. Andrew Kim are venerated. Saint Andrew Kim was a seminarian in Macao before he returned to Korea as the country's first Catholic priest.

Julia and her companions from Korea in Macao (May 1997)

Julia and her companions from Korea in front of the facade of St. Paul's Church, the rest of which was destroyed by fire in 1835.

People waiting to hear Julia in Holy Rosary Church in Kowloon, Hong Kong (May 1997)

Father Francis Su concelebrating Mass with Fr. Francis Elsinger and Fr. Lam in the Chapel for the Disabled in Kowloon, Hong Kong. During this Mass, Julia saw the Blessed Mother appearing behind the altar and received a message from her. (May 25, 1997)

The faithful attending the Mass (May 25, 1997)

May 25, 1997
in Kowloon, Hong Kong

Julia wrote:

During a Mass at the Hong Kong Pastoral Care Center for the Disabled, the Blessed Mother appeared as the Mother of Mercy, wearing a blue mantle, holding a scapular in her left hand and an ivory-colored rosary in her right hand, and with a bright light surrounding her head. Soon her blue mantle turned into a white mantle. She stretched out her hands toward us, who were attending the Mass, and then put her two hands together for prayer. This happened during the Gospel reading from Matthew 28:16-20 about Our Lord, just before the Ascension, giving the mission to His disciples to spread His teachings to the ends of the world. The Blessed Mother was smiling beautifully and lovingly and began speaking:

The Blessed Mother:

Dear children! Remember that I am always with you wherever you may be in the world. Especially console the disabled by letting them know that I love them very much. The devil is so active, employing all the available means to topple you. However, remember that I am guarding and protecting you who are following me, and entrust yourselves totally to me with faith and trust.

I also want you to practice my messages of love. If you accept my words well and practice them in union with each other, my messages of love will spread to China also, they (the people in China) will accept the Lord, and their souls will change. Therefore, for the conversion of sinners and for peace in the world, pray and make reparations and do penance without ceasing.

Whenever you pray, I, your Heavenly Mother, pray with you. However, I cannot pray with you when you pray in selfish ways.

My beloved children! Always remember that the door of my Ark of Salvation, an ark larger than the universe, remains open and that I wish all the children in the world to come aboard the Ark and help me so that not only you but (other) sinners may also repent and gain Heaven. If you all live following my messages of love, the just anger of God the Father will be softened, and the Lord will be comforted. To all of you, I give a blessing in the Lord's Love.

While the Blessed Mother was speaking, powerful light radiated from above and shone upon everyone in the Mass.

On June 12, 1997, Bishop Paul Chang-Yeol Kim of the Cheju Diocese in Korea came to Naju. While he was praying before the Blessed Mother's statue together with Fr. Anthony Kim, Julia, and Rufino Park, Julia saw a powerful light radiating from the Crucifix above the Blessed Mother's statue and a large Eucharist descending. She stretched out her hands, but the Eucharist landed forcefully on the altar.

Bishop Kim saw the Eucharist and knelt immediately, exclaiming, "The Living Jesus!" He later blessed pilgrims in the Chapel with the Eucharist. (June 12, 1997)

The Eucharist was placed at the foot of the Blessed Mother's statue for adoration by pilgrims before It was moved to the Naju Parish Church and later to the Kwangju Archdiocesan Office at the instruction of Archbishop Youn.

The Eucharist which descended miraculously on June 12, 1997, had images of the Sacred Heart of Jesus pierced with thorns, from which two drops of blood are falling. The Heart was crowned with a small cross and flames of love.

Bishop Paul Kim and Fr. Gabriel Park, Pastor of Naju, praying before the Eucharist and the Blessed Mother's statue. (June 12, 1997)

An overnight prayer meeting in the Naju Gymnasium commemorating the 12th anniversary of the Blessed Mother's first weeping in Naju (June 30, 1997)

The Blessed Mother:

"My beloved children! I will let the light, love and grace from my Immaculate Heart overflow in all of you who came despite the long distance, seeking me, who has been imploring (you) with tears. In this dangerous, extremely dangerous age, you will surely see new buds sprouting even on the burnt ground, when you realize that this Mother is needed for all of you and you are following me. Upon all of you who have been invited to my great banquet, I bestow my love combined with God's blessing."

(June 30, 1997)

On August 27, 1997, while Fr. Spies and other pilgrims were praying the Rosary in the Chapel, the Eucharist suddenly descended from the Crucifix to the floor before Fr. Spies and Julia. Julia was in pains in reparation for the sins of abortion in the world. The descent of the Eucharist was recorded by two video cameras permanently mounted on the Chapel ceiling. The spot on the floor where the Eucharist landed has been giving off a sweet fragrance ever since.

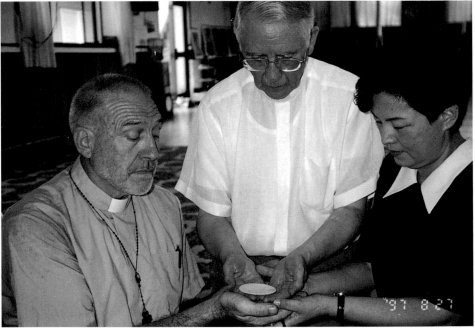

From left: Fr. Francis Elsinger of Hong Kong, Fr. Spies, and Julia, with the Eucharist that miraculously descended on August 27, 1997

Fr. Spies holding the Eucharist before the Blessed Mother's statue (August 27, 1997)

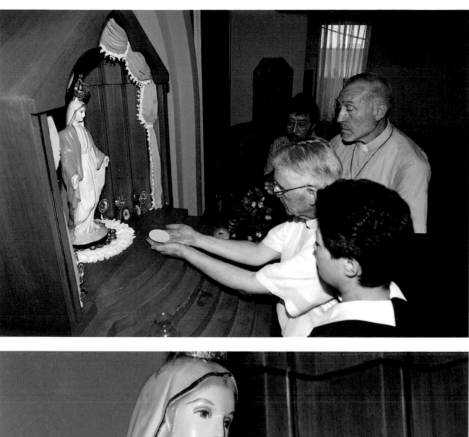

The Eucharist that descended on August 27, 1997, had exactly the same images as the One that descended two months earlier on June 12 during Bishop Paul Kim's visit.

The Eucharist that descended on August 27, 1997, was placed at the foot of the Blessed Mother's statue. It was later taken to the Kwangju Archdiocesan Office.

The Blessed Mother's Message on August 28, 1997

My beloved children who have been called! This Heavenly Mother's Heart is hurting so much, because the night in this world is becoming darker and the windows of the souls remain tightly closed despite the pleas by my Son Jesus and me to accept Us. This Mother's Heart is being torn apart into pieces, because those mistaken people do not see the plank in their own eyes but are trying to remove specks from others' with a hypocrisy that makes them criticize and judge others and concern themselves with external appearances only.

Because of the devil's schemes, division in the Church is becoming more severe and many souls are falling into a swamp and are struggling in it. But even many of the shepherds are incapable of discernment and are blaming others instead of rescuing them. I am so anxious.

My beloved children! Pray and pray for those who cannot see or hear, because they are blind and deaf. How can a blind person be a guide for other blind people? The sheep which follow a blind guide will all fall into a pit. Therefore, hurriedly open your eyes and ears and follow this Mother who has been imploring you with tears.

How overjoyed the devils will be, if those who have been given the task of feeding and taking care of others with the Word of God cannot hold on to the Heritage of Faith that has been entrusted to them?… Their responsibility before God is extremely heavy.

Know that my birth into this world was the signal announcing the fulfillment of all the covenants of the Old Testament and the arrival of a new era of all the graces and salvation in Christ. And practice the messages of love that I give you and be united to the Love of the Lord Who wills to save the world.

As the hands of a clock keep moving without pause, this world as well as all passions will pass away. But God's Commandments will never change. Therefore, have no fear, anxiety or despair, but entrust yourselves totally to this Mama who is bringing you up and cares about you. Do not forget that I, who share your sorrows, pains, anxieties and pains, am always with you. And more energetically and more courageously, make known to the whole world the Love that is flaming up in my Heart.

The days when the little souls gather, breathe and live in my Immaculate Heart are the days that are interspersed with my immense and powerful presence. Therefore, Satan, my enemy, may appear victorious now, but my Immaculate Heart will surely triumph with the help from you who look powerless and unworthy.

Therefore, all the children in the world! Stand up in a hurry and make a new start by combining your strength. When you work heroically, having complete loyalty and displaying the power of love, I will help you, comfort you and become not only your laurel crown in Heaven but your floral crown even while you live in the world.

Father Thomas More Jong-Pyo Chung, pastor of Kyerim-dong Church in Kwangju, meeting with pilgrims from Los Angeles (October 1997)

Julia embracing an elderly Vietnamese priest from the USA. This photo, taken on the Blessed Mother's mountain, shows a light shining down upon them.

2000

The Blessed Mother's Messages on June 13 and 18, 2000

My beloved children! My children who have been called because I love you extremely! With your help, I wish to build where Satan has destroyed, heal what Satan has injured, and achieve victory where Satan appears to have triumphed. Therefore, I want at least you, whom I have chosen, to abandon yourselves and offer up prayers of love of humble, little persons...

Remembering that the time of purification can be advanced or delayed depending on your prayers of deep love, pray with the undefeatable weapon which I gave you (which is a special grace by which one may have a generous heart and may love all with the combined Love of the Sacred Heart of Jesus and the Immaculate Heart of Mary. *See Our Lord's message on June 30, 1995.*) so that it (the time of purification) may come sooner than later. Then, the world will be reformed through a chain reaction more powerful than a nuclear reaction...

My beloved daughter! Tell my children who have been called. This Mother, who wishes that not even one among the children in the world be lost, is consoled by your offerings filled with love and devotion as you try to turn your whole life including even the most trivial things into prayers according to this Mother's wish.

This Mother, who shines light upon the road to Heaven as the Heavenly Prophetess, today offered up my beloved children whom I have called, on the altar of the Sacred Heart of Jesus which is burning with love. Therefore, become awakened so that you may not fall into despair or discouragement, and try to live the life of resurrection.

My little souls who have been called! Even if you are feeble and weak, offer yourselves up completely and become dissolved in my Immaculate Heart so that you may be united with my love and become one. Thus, if you become one, as the Father, the Son, and the Holy Spirit are One, respond to this Mother's wish to end violence and terror, saying *Amen*, and follow me, then Satan, who has been trying to conquer this world, will be defeated and run away and you will hold the victory banner of my burning Immaculate Heart and sing the glory of the Lord.

However, keeping in mind that, if you do not accept my words, I will be unable to help you, turn your life into prayers with a sublime heart and utmost devotion.

Our Lord's Message
on November 2, 2000
(All Souls' Day)

My beloved little soul! Thank you. Because of the increasing offenses against God by the children in the world, His wrath has reached an extreme level and has been overflowing little by little. It is eventually becoming like spilt water. Because of that, Satan is crying out for joy thinking that his work has reached the stage of success. However, God is delaying the cup of wrath because there are little souls like you.

That is because your turning your life into prayers, which you have been imploring (others to practice) and which is to offer up totally and turn into prayers everything from the moment you wake up to the moment you fall asleep, not neglecting even little and trivial things, becomes dissolved in My Sacred Heart and My Mother's Immaculate Heart and becomes one (with Them); it pulls out the nails one after another which the children of the world have driven into Me by offending (Me); and it becomes prayers of consolation that wipe away My Mother Mary's tears and tears of blood.

For this reason, Satan mobilizes all the available means to ceaselessly and ferociously attack to kill you, who are an apostle of My Sacred Heart and My Mother Mary's Immaculate Heart as well as an apostle of the Eucharist, as they consider you their enemy.

Therefore, become awake and pray more, bearing in mind that there is no time to be complacent, to pause, or to hesitate. When the cup of wrath comes down, many people will go the way of perdition because of all kinds of disasters that befall them suddenly and unexpectedly. However, all the children who seek Me through My Mother with their hearts widely open, even if they are the most evil sinners, will receive the grace of repentance. When they practice the messages of love, which are the key to the shortcut to Heaven, they will receive the cup of blessing instead of the cup of wrath; will live in joy, love and peace; and, on the last day, will possess the tree of eternal life which Adam and Eve lost.

(continued...)

My little soul! It is a pain greater than the pains of the suffering and death on the Cross to be scourged and crucified by the children, clergy, and religious who have been called. How many are the clergy, religious, and children who stand close to Me, Who is Love Itself, follow Me, and make Me known?

Ah, Ah! (I am) lonely and sad…

I showed the change in (the species of) the Eucharist several times and also came down personally through the Eucharist several times in order to give the totality of My Love to many children who come seeking My Mother and to share that Love with them. Nevertheless, the Eucharist, which is My substance, has been ignored and rejected with theories and reasoning. Instead of helping (people) experience My Love and Presence and making these known, the Eucharist has been judged to be (merely) a host and has become isolated. What else can this be other than a second death (for Me)?…

All the children in the world who have been called! It is not too late yet. Hurriedly come to Me, Who is Love Itself and the merciful Redeemer, without any fear and holding the hands of My Mother, who is the shortcut for coming to Me.

Even most of the children who say that they make Me known and love Me are spiritually blind and deaf. They have become spiritually disabled, lost their sense of direction, become confused, lost their balance, fallen into chaos, and are wandering and walking on the road to hell. I feel extremely sad and painful in My Heart, as if it is becoming torn apart into pieces.

My little souls who have been chosen through My Mother! At least you, remembering that only My Mother can turn God's wrath away from you, respond with *"Amen"* to My Mother's messages of love which she has earnestly given you, personally revealing her presence, love, and friendship with her tears, tears of blood, and fragrant oil; and, with total faith and trust, help all the herds of sheep, which have lost their way and are wandering, come aboard Mary's Ark of Salvation which My Mother has prepared and help them arrive at the heavenly harbor.

While making Me and My Mother known, you will also be persecuted in this world, but, in the next world, you will receive the power and privilege to pick and eat the fruits of the tree of eternal life, be given a share (of the heavenly inheritance), receive a shiny royal crown, and sing *Alleluia* at the side of Me and My Mother, together with the Saints, surrounded and guarded by the Angels, and enwrapped in glory.

The Blessed Mother's Mountain

Entrance to the Blessed Mother's mountain. About half an hour's drive from Naju.

The landscape of this mountain was designed according to a vision the Blessed Mother showed to Julia.

Pilgrims collecting water from the miraculous spring on the Blessed Mother's mountain.

The Stations of the Cross on the Blessed Mother's mountain

Our Lady of Naju for the World

Thanks to the dedicated efforts by many individuals, the Blessed Mother's messages and signs in Naju are becoming known all over the world. The messages have been translated into many languages and are still being translated into even more. The following are some photographs taken at meetings to hear the Blessed Mother's messages from Naju and to honor her replica statue.

A Mass in honor of Our Lady of Naju at St. Joseph's Church in Honolulu, Hawaii. There was an intense fragrance of roses in the church. (March 20, 1995)

Parishioners of Our Lady of Guadalupe Church in Texas honoring the replica statue of Our Lady of Naju (February 1995)

At St. Bridget's Church in Las Vegas, Nevada. People smelled the fragrance of roses.
(November 1994)

Father Garfield Jansen in India with a replica statue of Our Lady of Naju. The large
photographs of Our Lady of Naju Fr. Jansen received shed tears.

Father Fausto Zelaya of Irkutsk, Turkey, celebrating Mass in Menlo Park, California, in honor of Our Lady of Naju. He visited Naju in 1999.

People in Zambia, Africa, gathered to watch a video on Naju, **Mary Draws Us to the Eucharist,** *held by one of the boys. (February 2000)*

Appendix

Church Teachings on the Eucharist

Christ becomes present in the Sacrament of the Altar by the transformation of the whole substance of the bread into His Body and of the whole substance of the wine into His Blood (Council of Trent—DS #1641; *Catechism of the Catholic Church* #1376).

Christ is present whole and entire in each of the species and whole and entire in each of their parts, in such a way that the breaking of the bread does not divide Christ (Council of Trent—DS #1642; *Catechism of the Catholic Church* #1377).

The Body and the Blood of Christ together with His Soul and His Divinity and therefore the Whole Christ are truly present in the Eucharist (Council of Trent—DS #1651; *Catechism of the Catholic Church* #1374).

The Worship of Adoration *(latria)* must be given to Christ present in the Eucharist (Council of Trent—DS #1656; *Catechism of the Catholic Church* #1378).

The chief fruit of the Eucharist is an intrinsic union of the recipient with Christ (Council of Florence—DS #1320; *Catechism of the Catholic Church* #1391).

For the worthy reception of the Eucharist the state of grace as well as the proper and pious disposition are necessary (Council of Trent—DS #1667; *Catechism of the Catholic Church* #1385).

Also, Canon Law #919 (1): One who is to receive the Most Holy Eucharist is to abstain from any food or drink, with the exception only of water and medicine, for at least the period of one hour before Holy Communion.

Church Teaching on Miracles

If anyone shall have said that miracles are not possible, and hence that all accounts of them, even those contained in Sacred Scripture, are to be banished among the fables and myths; or, that miracles can never be known with certitude, and that the divine origin of the Christian religion cannot be correctly proved by them: let him be anathema. (The First Vatican Council, 1869-1870, DS #3034)

St. Thomas Aquinas on Eucharistic Miracles

It sometimes happens that such apparition comes about not merely by a change wrought in the beholders, but by an appearance which really exists outwardly. And this indeed is seen to happen when it is beheld by everyone under such an appearance, and it remains so not for an hour, but for a considerable time; and, in this case some think that it is the proper species of Christ's body. Nor does it matter that sometimes Christ's entire body is not seen there, but part of His flesh, or else that it is not seen in youthful guise, but in the semblance of a child, because it lies within the power of a glorified body for it to be seen by a non-glorified eye either entirely or in part, and under its own semblance or in strange guise.

While the dimensions remain the same as before, there is a miraculous change wrought in the other accidents, such as shape, color, and the rest, so that flesh, or blood, or a child is seen. And as was said already, this is not deception, because it is done to represent the truth, namely, to show by this miraculous apparition that Christ's body and blood are truly in this sacrament.

—St. Thomas Aquinas, **Summa Theologica**, *Part III, Question 76: Of the Way in Which Christ is in This Sacrament, Article 8*

Some of the Miraculous Changes in the Species of the Eucharist in Church History

1. Lanciano, Italy, Eighth Century—During a Mass celebrated by a priest-monk of the Order of St. Basil, who had some doubts about Our Lord's Real Presence in the Eucharist, as soon as he spoke the words of Consecration the host suddenly changed into a circle of flesh and the wine into visible blood.

2. Braine, France, 1153—During the Mass celebrated by Archbishop Anculphe de Pierrefonds, people saw, instead of the Host, a small child. Vastly moved by this miracle, many of the non-Catholics who had come to the Mass for curiosity demanded Baptism.

3. Ferrara, Italy, 1171—During a Mass on March 28, Easter Sunday, concelebrated by Padre Pietro de Verona and three other priests, a stream of blood suddenly spurted from the Host when the consecrated Host was broken into two parts.

4. Augsburg, Germany, 1194—A woman in Augsburg removed the Host from her mouth after receiving Holy Communion with the intention of reserving a consecrated Host in her home. She fashioned two pieces of wax, placed the Host between them and sealed the edges, thereby creating a crude reliquary. After keeping the Blessed Sacrament in her home for five years, her conscience was so troubled that in 1199 she informed her parish priest of this. The priest visited her home and returned the Host to the Church. When the wax reliquary was opened, it was found that part of the Host had changed into flesh.

5. Santarem, Portugal, early Thirteenth Century—A woman, who lived in Santarem, thirty-five miles south of Fatima, was misled by a sorceress, and removed the Host from her mouth and wrapped it in her veil, intending to take it to the sorceress. But within a few moments, blood began to issue from the Host. The amount of blood increased so much that it dripped from the cloth and attracted the attention of bystanders. After approbation by church authorities, it was recognized as a miracle.

6. Bolsena-Orvieto, Italy, 1263—A German priest stopped at Bolsena while on a pilgrimage to Rome. Even though he was a pious priest, he found it difficult to believe that Christ was actually present in the consecrated Host. While celebrating Mass, he had barely spoken the words of Consecration when blood started to seep from the consecrated Host and trickle over his hands onto the altar and the corporal.

7. Siena, Italy, 1330—A farmer of a village on the outskirts of Siena became grievously ill and sent for the priest. In great haste the priest removed a consecrated Host from the tabernacle, but instead of placing it in a pyx, he inserted the Host between the pages of his breviary and hurried to the bedside of the farmer. When he opened the breviary to give the Host to the sick man, he discovered that the Host was bloody and almost melted.

(Source: **Eucharistic Miracles***, Joan Carroll Cruz, Tan Books & Publishers, 1987)*

Some of the Miraculous Receptions of the Eucharist in Church History

1. St. Clement, Bishop of Ancyra (Fourth Century), received Communion from Our Lord, while in prison awaiting martyrdom.
2. St. Bonaventure (d. 1274) received Communion from an angel.
3. St. Catherine of Siena (d. 1380) received Communion from Our Lord and also from angels.
4. St. Pascal Babylon (d. 1592) received Communion from an angel on many occasions.
5. St. Mary Magdalen de Pazzi (d. 1607) received Communion directly from Our Lord.
6. In Fatima, St. Michael the Archangel brought a chalice and a Sacred Host to the three children (1917).
7. The Eucharist miraculously appeared on the tongue of Therese Neumann (d. 1962) on numerous occasions.

(Source: **Eucharistic Miracles**, *Joan Carroll Cruz, Tan Books & Publishers, 1987)*

The Last Supper for the Third Passover?
A message from the Blessed Mother in Naju
keeps echoing in my mind
By Il-Kyu Park

(Mr. Park was formerly the president of a Korean company in Japan and is a well-respected Catholic lay leader in Korea and Japan. He wrote this article in Summer 1997)

What is the Last Supper? It is a banquet of love and sharing. In order to give the totality of my love, which is so high, deep and wide, to my beloved Pope, Cardinals, Bishops, priests, religious and all my children in the world, together with my Son Jesus, I am squeezing all of myself and giving them fragrance and oil. The fragrance and oil that I give for the sake of all are gifts from God and represent my presence, love and friendship.
—*The Blessed Mother's message on April 8, 1993, Holy Thursday*

It has been revealed in the Holy Scripture that there are three kinds of exoduses which are related to each other in the synthesis of God's plans and providence for the salvation of the human race:

1. the exodus from Egypt to the Promised Land led by Moses;
2. the exodus from sufferings and death to the glorious Resurrection accomplished by Christ; and
3. the exodus of the Church from the sinful world to a new heaven and a new earth.

The Blessed Mother's statue exudes fragrant oil from the top of hear head. An image of the Eucharist also appeared in her right hand. (April 1993)

The first two have been accomplished already. In fact, they are the signs and promises that precede the final exodus. It can be said that all Christians—the Apostles, the Saints, priests, religious and laity are marching toward this singular goal: the third exodus. Of course, this third exodus is totally dependent on the merits of Christ. It can be thought of as an unfolding application of the merits of His redemptive suffering to the deliverance of the world from evil.

It was June 12, 1994, when I first visited Naju. Mr. Bernard from Switzerland, working at a retreat house in Japan, introduced me to Fr. Raymond Spies. Then, Fr. Spies directed me to Naju. The Blessed Mother's statue in Naju that I first saw was blue and white in color and had a height of about 50 cm. It looked like an ordinary statue that one could easily find elsewhere.

This was the statue that was widely known for tears and tears of blood. But on the day of my visit, there were no traces of tears. I looked more closely and saw streams of oil from the left side of her head, flowing down on her forehead, both sides of her left eye, and her left cheek, reflecting light in the Chapel. I was not sure if it was from the oil, but the area around the statue and, actually, the whole Chapel was filled with quite a strong fragrance of roses, which one could easily smell even without paying attention. On June 14, two priests and about thirty other pilgrims from Japan arrived together with Fr. Spies. It was almost noon when Julia also came out, and the atmosphere in the Chapel became quite animated. Some people were on their knees, praying the Rosary, and others were taking photos in front of the Blessed Mother's statue. Julia was talking mostly with priests. She looked like a usual mother in a rural town, who seemed to have worked at a barley mill. I also took photographs with others and exchanged greetings. I had a long talk with Fr. Luige de Rucoru, an elderly theologian, about the Blessed Mother until we parted with each other.

Several weeks later, I received some gifts from Fr. de Rucoru and Mr. Goga, an elderly layman in Japan, both of whom I had met in Naju. Fr. de Rucoru surprised me by sending 257 volumes of books, mostly on the Blessed Mother, and Mr. Goga sent me a small package containing several photographs taken on the day of their visit to Naju and a letter written politely with a brush. The three packages of books from Fr. de Rucoru were heavy and were sent by sea mail. They were very surprising and rare gifts. But let me move on to the subject of the other package that may be even more surprising.

There were two identical photographs among others that Mr. Goga, sent me. They were two identical prints of a photograph of the Blessed Mother's statue which was exuding fragrant oil. I could not understand why Mr. Goga included these two same photos in the package. Anyhow, these two photos were nicely wrapped in transparent vinyl bags just like other photos. What was surprising was that only these two photos were wet with some clear oil. How is this possible? What happened? Oil flows from photographs, from dry paper, as if the paper was alive?... I observed this for several days, but it was a certain fact. My family and other people also confirmed this. Several days later, I went down to Naju and showed these photographs to Julia in her living room. As soon as she received the photos in her hands, the room became filled with a powerful fragrance of roses. The fragrance was spreading even to the outside of the room. Some of the volunteer workers were surprised and rushed into the room. They said that this oil was identical to the oil that was exuding from the Blessed Mother's statue. When Mr. Goga heard about this, he carefully examined an identical photograph that he was keeping in his album but could not find anything unusual. Why is the Blessed Mother giving this gift of her fragrant oil and fragrance through these photos only to me? Is the Blessed Mother really giving her fragrant oil and fragrance as a special gift for me? What do this fragrance and fragrant oil mean? Anyhow, there has been no change in this fragrance and fragrant oil even now, three years after it began. Many people know about this.

At the beginning of this writing, I quoted the sentence from the messages in Naju: What is the Last Supper? "The Last Supper"—this term appears once in the Old Testament and once in the New Testament. In Exodus 12:11, *"Thus you shall eat it: you shall gird your reins, and you shall have shoes on your feet, holding staves in your hands, and you shall eat in haste."* This meal refers to the last supper that the Israelites shared with each other before leaving Egypt. In the New Testament, the meal refers to the Last Supper that Our Lord shared with His disciples as the Passover meal before His arrest.

The Last Supper that was shared as the Passover meal! These are not the words of someone who is unfamiliar with the Scriptures. Rather, they are the words of someone who penetrates both the Old Testament and the New Testament. *"What is the Last Supper?"* Who can dare ask this question and give a clear answer? The Blessed Mother is giving us a teaching of profound significance and high intensity by means of her message through Julia in Naju on April 8, 1993, and through Fr. Stefano Gobbi on April 13, 1995, both of which were the Feast of the Priesthood in commemoration of the Lord's establishment of the Sacraments of the Holy Eucharist and Holy Orders, on the profound meaning of the Last Supper that is to be shared as the Passover meal. In her message through Fr. Gobbi, the Blessed Mother quotes from the Bible, *"I have eagerly desired to eat this Passover meal with you before I suffer,"* and also says, *"The entire life of Jesus was destined toward this sublime and irreversible moment,"* and *"Jesus has been walking toward that pinnacle every day."* She repeatedly emphasizes, *"Jesus has always desired to reach the point where His Passover is completed."* She again reminds us of the words in the Gospel: *"I have eagerly desired to eat this Passover meal with you before I suffer."* With these words of profound significance, she awakens us to the meaning of "the Last Supper" and says, *"The hour that Jesus has desired so eagerly in this end time has begun. That is because, with His merciful Love, He is preparing the greatest victory."* In conclusion, she says, *"Therefore, you too should desire eagerly to eat this Passover meal before suffering."*

What is then the third Passover meal of this age that the Blessed Mother is asking us to desire eagerly and share with each other? During the first Passover before leaving Egypt, the meal that the Israelites shared in haste, with reins on their waist, shoes on their feet, and staves in their hands, was the meat of lambs, unleavened bread and bitter herbs. During the second Passover, the meal that the Lord shared with His disciples as the Last Supper before His arrest was bread and wine turned into Christ's Body and Blood. Then, what is the meal during the third Passover of this age, which the Blessed Mother asked us to eagerly desire in her words through Fr. Gobbi? I believe that a very clear and perfect answer to that question can be found in the words from the Blessed Mother's message through Julia Hong Sun Yoon Kim on April 8, 1993, which was quoted at the beginning of this writing. I have read the messages of Naju ten times so far, searching for the meaning of the fragrance and fragrant oil from the simple photographs of Our Lady's statue that I received as gifts. I would like to point out, with a deep sense of caution and humility, to the Church and the faithful the meaning of these words in the messages that I have found, filled with profound gratitude and love.

> *What is the Last Supper? It is a banquet of love and sharing. In order to give the totality of my love, which is high, deep and wide, to my beloved Pope, Cardinals, Bishops, priests, religious and all my children in the world, together with my Son Jesus, I am squeezing all of myself and giving them fragrance and oil.*

The Last Supper is a banquet of love and sharing, and she is squeezing all of herself to give the fragrance and the fragrant oil to all—from the Pope to the children in the world—so that they may share it with one another.

The Last Supper during the second Passover was the Lord's Body and Blood. Then, the Passover meal that we are to share as the Last Supper during this third Passover is the fragrance and fragrant oil that the Blessed Mother personally gives us by squeezing herself. Then, it would not be difficult to infer that it is the Blessed Mother who is leading us in the third Passover. If one thinks that some logical jump, exaggeration or rash judgment is included in this reasoning, more discussion will be necessary. Continuing the reasoning, God, Yahweh, led His people through Moses during the first Passover and Christ led the second Passover. Then, it becomes clear that the third Passover, which will transform this sinful world into a new heaven and a new earth which will be with the Lord, will be led by the Blessed Virgin Mary, who is a created being but is elevated to the Divine Motherhood and is the Second Eve, as mentioned in the Proto-Gospel (Genesis 3:15). When one has an open mind, free from prejudice, it will be clear beyond doubt that the above-quoted message in Naju is a solemn declaration of the Last Supper and a marching order to her beloved Church and the human race during the third Passover. Therefore, I think that not only the Catholic Church in Korea but also the Holy Father and the whole Church need to humbly and attentively listen to what is summarily contained in these words.

When the Lord was being rejected in Nazareth, He said the following words which are terribly frightening to us:

> *During the time of Elijah when the heaven was closed and there was a severe drought for three-and-a-half years there were many widows in Israel. But Elijah was sent not to others but only to a widow living in Sarebda in Sidon. There were many lepers in Israel at the time of Prophet Elijah. But among them only a Syrian was cured.*

How should we understand these words of the Lord? As God chose the Blessed Mother, the Blessed Mother can choose Naju and Julia. Shouldn't we remind ourselves that it is God, the Lord, and the Blessed Mother Who choose according to Their Will? Shouldn't all of us fear God, know how to humbly bend our own will, follow God's Will, and truly serve Him? Shouldn't we thus stand on a beautiful and good foundation that is unshakable? I think that we all must keep in mind the Lord's Words, *"We are unprofitable servants; we have done what we were obliged to do"* (Luke 17:10), follow the Holy Father, become liberated from the sense of vested rights, and, thus, return to this very free and fragrant place for accepting God's Words.

I look back at what the Lord did two thousand years ago. He first changed water into wine, then, finally shared the Last Supper with His disciples and, then, was arrested to complete His Death. He shed His Precious Blood on the Cross as the Victim for all, and, finally, overcame Death, opened the gate of the tomb, and came out.

I also look back at what the Blessed Mother has done in Naju. First she showed her tears, then, tears of blood, then, fragrance and oil, and then, the Eucharistic signs. Unlike any other apparition sites in Church history, these signs were given in powerful ways, one after another, regardless of the world's responses. Now, the Last Supper is nearing its end. Doesn't this mean that there only remains the Passion and the Death, which will lead to the glorious Resurrection?

Let us listen again to the solemn declaration of the Last Supper that the Blessed Virgin Mary is making to the Holy Father and all the children in the world of this age:

> *What is the Last Supper? It is a banquet of love and sharing. In order to give the totality of my love, which is high, deep and wide, to my beloved Pope, Cardinals, Bishops, priests, religious and all my children in the world, together with my Son Jesus, I am squeezing all of myself and giving them fragrance and oil. The fragrance and oil that I give to all are gifts from God and represent my presence, love and friendship.*

There are several words in the above message that demand special attention: *"together with my Son Jesus."* At the climax of the second Passover, namely, during the Crucifixion, the Blessed Mother was standing, as the Co-Redemptrix, with the Apostle John at the side of the Lord hanging on the Cross. Likewise, this time, the Lord is standing at the side of the Blessed Mother, who is leading us in the third Passover, by giving us the fragrance and oil as the food by squeezing all of herself.

> *The fragrance and oil that I give to all are gifts from God and represent my presence, love and friendship.*

This means that God is giving to this world in this age the presence of the Blessed Mother as His gift of love. As He gave His Only Son as the gift during the second Passover, He is giving the Blessed Mother, who is a descendant of Eve and is strengthened at the foot of her Son's Cross, as a gift to the Holy Father and all the people of this age. She will not fall into the serpent's temptation; rather, she will crush his head. It means a majestic accomplishment of God's Will to rescue the human race, which was lost because of the weak and immature Eve, through the Blessed Mother, who is a creature but is elevated to the Divine Motherhood. We can surmise that God wills to achieve a more precious and glorious victory through the Blessed Virgin Mary, a descendant of Eve whom He created with love as *"the bone of his (Adam's) bone and the flesh of his flesh,"* instead of achieving the victory Himself.

The Blessed Mother herself clarifies her mission:

> *Today focus your eyes on this Heavenly Mother, who is enwrapped with the extremely pure light of the Paschal joy and is again declaring in a quiet and motherly way His glorious return to you.*
>
> —Her message through Fr. Gobbi on April 7, 1996

We can clearly see from His life on earth that the Lord does not flatter or compromise with the world or with any other existing force that goes against His Will. As she chose little children and spoke through them in Lourdes and Fatima, I think that the Blessed Mother can choose a poor country woman to make a solemn pronouncement of the Last Supper of the third Passover that will conclude an era to the whole world.

As he drew near, he saw the city (Jerusalem) and wept over it, saying, "If this day you only knew what makes for peace—but now it is hidden from your eyes. For the days are coming upon you when your enemies will raise a palisade against you; they will encircle you and hem you in on all sides. They will smash you to the ground and your children within you, and they will not leave one stone upon another within you because you did not recognize the time of your visitation." (Luke 19:41-44)

How wonderful it would be, if everyone in this age can listen to these Words of the Lord as a warning!

I would like to end this writing by quoting the words of St. John suggesting to all that we listen to the loud voice from the throne in Heaven, as the revelations were approaching the end:

Behold, God's tabernacle is among men. He will dwell with them and they will be his people and God himself will always be with them. (Revelation 21:3)

There are the Blessed Mother's tears and her tears of blood. There are her fragrance and oil. There are her words that formed a book. As if trying to liberate the whole human race from the bondage of exile caused by the old serpent, seven times she has solemnly manifested her Son Jesus (in the Eucharist), Whom she was carrying in her womb, as we have always prayed for. Then, even if that place is a poor cottage in a small town, we must all know that it is God's tabernacle among us on earth and a dwelling place of the Blessed Virgin Mary who was conceived immaculately.

According to her Son's request while He was hanging on the Cross and shedding blood for our sake, the Blessed Mother is trying to gather all her children of this age who are like John the Apostle in her Immaculate Heart by squeezing herself and giving them fragrance and oil. I wish to ask everyone to open their eyes and recognize the Mother at the banquet of love and to participate in and walk at the head of the journey from this loveless, dry desert to the new heaven and new earth that will be opened with God's Love, instead of falling behind.

Professor Dietrich von Hildebrand On True Renewal in the Church

False alternatives

When one reads the luminous encyclical *Ecclesiam Suam* of Pope Paul VI or the magnificent "Dogmatic Constitution on the Church" of the Fathers of the Council, one cannot but realize the greatness of the Second Vatican Council.

But when one turns to so many contemporary writings—some by very famous theologians, some by minor ones, some by laymen offering us their dilettante theological concoctions—one can only be deeply saddened and even filled with grave apprehension. For it would be difficult to conceive a greater contrast than that between the official documents of Vatican II and the superficial, insipid pronouncements of various theologians and laymen that have broken out everywhere like an infectious disease.

On the one side, we find the true spirit of Christ, the authentic voice of the Church; we find texts that in both form and content breathe a glorious supernatural atmosphere. On the other hand, we find a depressing secularization, a complete loss of the *sensus supernaturalis*, a morass of confusion.

The distortion of the authentic nature of the Council produced by this epidemic of theological dilettantism expresses itself chiefly in the false alternatives between which we are all commanded to choose: either to accept the secularization of Christianity or to deny the authority of the Council...

The teachings of the false prophets

...He is a false prophet who denies original sin and mankind's need of redemption and thereby undermines the meaning of Christ's death on the Cross. He is not a true Christian who no longer sees that redemption of the world through Christ is the source of true happiness and that nothing can be compared to this one glorious fact.

He is a false prophet who no longer accepts the absolute primacy of the first commandment of Christ—to love God above all things—and who claims that our love of God can manifest itself exclusively in our love of neighbor. He is a false prophet who no longer understands that to long for the *I-Thou* union with Christ and for transformation in Christ is the very meaning of our life. He is a false prophet who claims that morality reveals itself not primarily in man's relationship with God, but in those things that concern human welfare. And he has fallen prey to the teaching of false prophets who only sees in the wrong done our neighbor our injury to him and remains blind to the offense against God that this wrong implies. He who no longer sees the radical difference that exists between charity and humanitarian benevolence has become deaf to the message of Christ.

He who is more impressed and thrilled by "cosmic processes," "evolution," and the speculations of science than by the reflection of Christ's Sacred Humanity in a Saint and by the victory over the world that the very existence of a Saint embodies, is no longer filled with Christian spirit. He who cares more for the earthly welfare of humanity than for its sanctification has lost the Christian view of the universe.

True renewal calls us to transformation in Christ

...This third choice is based on unshakable faith in Christ and in the infallible magisterium of His Holy Church. It takes it for granted that there is no room for change in the divinely revealed doctrine of the Church. It admits no possibility of change except that development of which Cardinal Newman speaks:

the explicit formulation of what was implicit in the faith of the Apostles or of what necessarily follows from it.

This attitude holds that the Christian morality of holiness, the morality revealed in the Sacred Humanity of Christ and His commandments and exemplified in all the saints, remains forever the same. It holds that being transformed in Christ, becoming a new creature in Him, is the goal of our existence. In the words of St. Paul, "This is the will of God, your sanctification" (1 Thess. 4:3).

This position maintains that there is a radical difference between the kingdom of Christ and the *saeculum* (world); it takes into account the struggle between the spirit of Christ and the spirit of Satan through all the centuries past and to come, until the end of the world. It believes that Christ's words are as valid today as in any former time: "Had you been of the world, the world would love its own; but as you are not of the world, as I have chosen you out of the world, the world hates you" (John 15:19).

Renewal restores the supernatural vitality of the Church

The process of renewal is a shedding of secularizing influences which, because of human frailty and the trends and tendencies of an era, have slipped into the practice of the Church and the religious life of the faithful.

As such, it is the very opposite of an evolution or progression. Rather, it is a returning to the essential and authentic spirit of the Church, a process of purification and restoration. It is a dramatic manifestation of the war between the spirit of the world (in the meaning of the Gospels) and the Spirit of Christ— which St. Augustine described as the *battle of the two cities*. In this process all views and practices that are incompatible with Christ are continually eliminated. Such was the reform of St. Gregory VII; such were the reforms of numerous Councils, especially the Council of Trent.

...But the Church also has a human, natural aspect. Insofar as it is a human institution composed of frail men, it, too, is exposed to the influence of this alternating rhythm of history. Therefore the Church has the continual mission of rejecting all such influences and presenting anew to humanity the untarnished plentitude of divine truth and authentic Christian life—that is, the real message of Christ to all men.

(From **Trojan Horse in the City of God** by Professor Dietrich von Hildebrand published by Sophia Institute Press, 1993)

"The Grace of God has not been in vain"
A priest in South Africa works hard to promote Our Lady's messages

January 5, 2000

Beloved in Christ,

Happy New Year and compliments of the season. As we begin the 3rd millennium, I ask the good Lord to renew your strength.

Some time ago, I promised to send you a report on what I am doing here in order to promote the Marian messages to Julia. I am doing it from personal conviction that the messages of love which God is offering to everyone of us at this time through our Mother Mary via Julia is proper to our time. Secondly, the miraculous phenomena (Sacred hosts descending, statue shedding tears and tears of blood, Sacred host turning into visible flesh, etc.) provide solid backing to the Church's teaching on the Eucharist. Granted that we must not crave for signs and miracles, we must, however, be grateful to God when he decides to give some signs.

From the video: "Mary draws us to the Eucharist," the book on Messages of love and other materials which you freely sent to me, I worked out a series of talks on the Eucharist and Reconciliation. I give the talks and show the film "Mary draws us to the Eucharist." I gave the talk and showed the film once to my parishioners, and since then I have been receiving invitations from parishes far and near requesting me to come and talk on the Eucharist and show them the film. The feedback I have been receiving from such talks has been fantastic. In some places, I noticed some people going to the Blessed Sacrament to adore immediately after the talks. Some come right away to me to ask for confessions. Personally, I observed some people shedding tears as I give some of the messages of love. I interpret some of those tears as tears of repentance. As St. Paul would say, the grace of God has not been in vain as I go round the parishes to talk to the people about the messages of love which God is giving in our time.

In October, I talked to over 150 young people who gathered for vocation rally in our pastoral region. On the 6th/12/1999, I talked to over 750 members of the Sacred Heart of Jesus solidarity and showed them the film "Mary draws us to the Eucharist." On the 13/12/1999, I talked to over 100 youth gathered for their annual bible quiz competition which I organised. The talk and the film made a deep impression on them. My prayer is that God will draw many more people to the Eucharist and to the Sacrament of Reconciliation. A German visitor who listened to my talk on the Eucharist came to me and said a few encouraging words. Could you send me the address of the person in charge of organising the pilgrimage to Naju.

Be assured of my prayerful support. Wishing you the best in this new year.

Yours in JMJ,

Fr. Godwin Nnadozie, MSP.
St. Mary's Catholic Church
Mafikeng, North West Province, South Africa

Letter from Archbishop Marcello Zago, OMI, Secretary of the Sacred Congregation for the Evangelization of Peoples, in the Holy See

CONGREGATIO
PRO GENTIUM EVANGELIZATIONE

20 August 1998

3024/98
Prot.............................

Dear Mr. Sang M. Lee and family,

Herewith I acknowledge receipt of your letter of June 8, 1998, together with some recent publications concerning Naju.

The Congregation for the Evangelization of Peoples has carefully studied the material forwarded by you and wishes to thank you for this communication.

You may be assured that this Congregation is well aware of the questions concerning Naju as well as of the problems touching upon the faith and the form of christian life in Corea and elsewhere, in the wake of Vatican Council II.

You are invited to pray that the Holy Spirit may enlighten all the persons of the Church whose duty it is to watch over the purity of the faith. Following the guidance of the Corean Bishops' Conference, it is hoped that the faithful of the much admired Church in Corea will hold fast to the true catholic faith and practice, without being perturbed by doubtful statements of some individuals. Relying on the divine grace of the Holy Spirit and the unfailing help of the Blessed Mother, the present problems will certainly be overcome.

Imploring upon you and all the faithful of the Catholic Church in Corea God's abundant blessings,
I am devotedly yours in the Lord

+ Marcello Zago omi
   Secr.

Mr. **Sang M. Lee and family**
Mary's Touch by Mail
P.O. Box 1668
Gresham, OR 97030
U.S.A.

Available Publications

Books

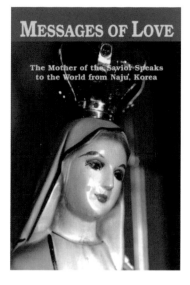

Messages of Love—The Mother of the Savior Speaks to the World from Naju, Korea All the messages that Julia Kim in Naju, Korea, received from Our Lord and Our Lady between July 1985 and January 1996, plus two booklets (at no extra charge) containing more recent messages. 304 pages, including about 60 B&W photos.

Price: $12.95 plus $3 S&H

(A Spanish edition of this book, Mensajes de Amor, is available at the same price.)

Our Lady's Messages from Naju — Compiled according to subject
A selection of the messages that Julia Kim in Naju received from Our Lord and Our Lady, compiled according to about 100 different subjects. Helpful for understanding the major themes of the messages more clearly. 112 pages including 13 B&W photos.
Price: $3.95 plus $2.50 S&H

The Reality of the Living Presence — Eucharistic Miracle in Naju, Korea
 By Fr. Joseph P. Finn, Ph.D., of London, Ontario, Canada, who, together with Bishop Roman Danylak, witnessed a Eucharistic miracle in Naju, Korea on September 22, 1995. Fr. Finn sets forth his experiences, discusses possible responses, and some theological aspects of the miracle. 32 pages, including 10 color photos. Size: 4 x 6˝"
Price: $2.50 plus $1 S&H

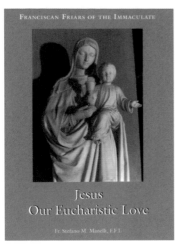

Jesus Our Eucharistic Love —
Eucharistic Life Exemplified by the Saints
By Fr. Stefano M. Manelli, F.F.I., S.T.D.
A masterpiece on Eucharistic devotion.
Fr. Manelli founded "Casa Mariana" (House
of Mary) under the inspiration of St.
Maximilian Kolbe's idea of the City of the
Immaculate. In this book, he explains how to
know, love and live the Eucharist. 128 pages.
Price: $5.00 plus $2.50 S&H

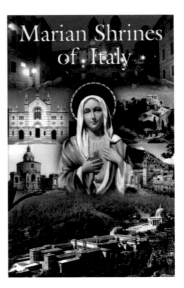

Marian Shrines of Italy
Published by Franciscan Friars of the
Immaculate, New Bedford, Massachusetts.
Represents 35 of the 1,500 Marian Shrines
of Italy. Authored by over 15 experts and
well-known writers. A compendium of
2,000 years of Catholic culture in Italy. 178
pages, 155 illustrations (most in full color).
Price: $12.50 plus $3 S&H

A Handbook on Guadalupe
Published by Franciscan Friars of the
Immaculate. A collection of short,
interesting, in-depth articles which cover
the historical, biblical, liturgical, sociologi-
cal, devotional, and scientific evidence, etc.,
on the miraculous image and Our Lady's
message for our times. 244 pages,
50 illustrations (20 in color).
Price: $12.50 plus $3 S&H

Videos

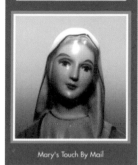

The Queen of the Holy Rosary in Naju, Korea
A comprehensive coverage of the supernatural signs and messages in Naju since their beginning in 1985. Scenes of the Blessed Mother weeping tears and tears of blood, fragrant oil exuding from her statue, Julia suffering the pains of the Crucifixion and of abortion, Eucharistic miracles, and more. VHS, 55 min.
Price: $14.95 plus $3 S&H

Mary Draws Us to the Eucharist (#1)
Actual video and photo footage of the Eucharistic miracles in Naju between June 1988 and July 1995. Powerful for defending the Church teachings on the Eucharist and revitalizing Eucharistic devotion among the faithful. VHS, 68 min.
Price: $15.95 plus $3 S&H

Mary Draws Us to the Eucharist (#2)
Eucharistic miracles through Julia Kim between September 1995 and August 1997, which includes a Eucharistic miracle in the Vatican on October 31, 1995, which was witnessed by the Holy Father. VHS, 72 min.
Price: $15.95 plus $3 S&H

Tears of Love

Our Heavenly Mother's Messages
from Naju, Korea

Tears of Love—Our Heavenly Mother's Messages from Naju, Korea
Scenes of Our Lady weeping tears and tears of blood through her statue in Naju; fragrant oil exuding from the same statue; miracles of the sun; Eucharistic miracle; and more. Readings of the selected messages from Our Lady in Naju. VHS, 62 min.

Price: $12.95 plus $3 S&H

A Pilgrimage to Naju, Korea
Some practical information for those who wish to make a pilgrimage to Naju and also video footage of previous pilgrimages. VHS, 58 min.

Price: $10.95 plus $3 S&H

Marian Conference in Long Beach, California, November 8, 1997
Scenes of the Marian Conference attended by Bishop Roman Danylak, Father Francis Su, Julia and Julio Kim, and others in the Convention Center in Long Beach, California. VHS, 96 min.

Price: $12.95 plus $3 S&H